Family·*ish'*

HOW TO RAISE A FABULOUS FAMILY

Geoffrey V. Dudley, Sr., Ph.D., D.Min

Family-ish': How to Raise a Fabulous Family

by Dr. Geoffrey V. Dudley, Sr., Ph.D., D.Min

Published by The Church Online, LLC

For information, address the publisher:

The Church Online, LLC

1000 Ardmore Blvd.

Pittsburgh, PA 15221

International Standard Book Number: 978-1-940786-67-4

Library of Congress Catalogue Card Number: Available Upon Request

Printed in the United States of America

First Edition: November 2021

Dedication

This book is dedicated to my loving parents, the late Bishop Lemon Dudley, Sr. and the late Mrs. Ida Dorothy Dudley. You instilled in me a love of God and family. I learned how to raise my family by the grace, intentionality, intimacy, empowerment, and lessons learned you instilled in me. Thanks Ma for the passion for family and thanks Daddy for the persistence to provide for my family. I miss and love you both!

I also want to dedicate this book to my family—Glenda, my wife for life; Mahogany and Geoffrey II, my loving, creative, and incredible children; and my talented son-in-law, Travis. Your lives have become priority and your support gives me life.

Acknowledgements

I would like to thank my loyal, creative, and smart executive assistant, Dagne. Nothing gets done in my ministry without your fingerprints all over it. Additionally, I would like to thank Anne—only you can decipher and type what I write.

Most of all, I want to thank my lovely wife, Glenda Dudley, of 36 years, and my amazing children Mahogany and Geoffrey II. Your contribution to this book is immeasurable. Thanks for your patience, your stories, and your support.

Table of Contents

Chapter 1

Welcome to the Fabulous Family

Let's talk about families. I have bad news, and I have good news.

The bad news is old news: families are hurting today.

The causes of pain are many. Disillusionment, devaluing, disintegration—just to begin with. Then there is promiscuity, cheating, disobedience to one's vows, divorce, physical abuse, drifting caused by too many choices, drug addiction, inadequate finances, absentee fathers, self-absorbed mothers, rambunctious children, lack of commitment, and media that put form in front of substance and act as pseudo parents that teach morals contrary to biblical norms.

The statistics are truly alarming. Fifty percent of first marriages end in divorce. Only thirty percent of millennials are married today. In 1960, the number for their age cohort would have been sixty percent. Millennials wait due to debt, self-absorption, or living together. Half of all children are born out of wedlock. Mental health issues for kids are on the rise. Over-medication of children is on the rise, and basic parenting is on the decline. Boys, especially, suffer from all kinds of problems. Violent video games become a preoccupation. Mothers are often devalued. People spend more time surfing the net and playing on their smartphones than focusing on their families. The financial picture is not rosy, either. Most families have less than five thousand dollars for retirement and are one paycheck away from complete devastation.

Nobody seems to have much direction today, and families are especially hard hit by this rudderless condition.

So, that is the bad news.

What's the good news?

There is a way forward for you and your family. You do not need to be content with a barely functional family. You can have a fully functional family, a fabulous family. Yes, you can!

How?

The answer is old and comes from God, as all good things do. A truly fabulous family is a covenant family!

What is a covenant family?

God established His covenant commitment when He established the first family, Adam and Eve, in the Garden of Eden. Ever since, God has enacted His will on the earth through families. Indeed, in the Book of Exodus, God identifies Himself with families: "Then he said, 'I am the God of your father, the God of Abraham, the God of Isaac and the God of Jacob.'" (Exodus 3:6, NIV).

After that, God established His will on the earth through families. In fact, the twelve tribes are a complex system of family ties: Reuben, Simeon, Levi, Judah, Issachar, Zebulun, Dan, Naphtali, Gad, Asher, Joseph, and Benjamin. While these are tribes, they are also groups of families. By making the Old Covenant with the people of Israel and giving them His laws, God made a covenant with families and gave them a code of family behavior. Family covenant is how God gets things done.

In the New Testament, Jesus updates and upgrades this biblical principle of working through families by having the Twelve Disciples represent the family system of the Old Testament. Jesus nurtures and develops the Apostles to continue this covenant relationship and work. This time, however, grace, which is another word for love, will be the core of the covenant inside of the law. Jesus prepared His family and dealt with His family dissent, disillusionment, and dysfunction. He then had His own family of disciples expand this family-covenant thinking to include the entire world.

The New Covenant is a promise made by God to families, but it is not a legalistic promise, like the one He made to the people of Israel in the Old Testament. Through Jesus' death on the cross, God promises to forgive sin and to be in fellowship with those who turn toward Him. At the Last Supper, Jesus said, "This cup is the new covenant in my blood, which is poured out for you" (Luke 22:20, NIV). This is a promise of love. It is also a promise of grace: "For sin shall no longer be your master, because you are not under the law, but under grace" (Romans 6:14, NIV). But just because the New Covenant is one of grace, one of the heart, and not one only of the law, that fact does not mean one can just go and do whatever one wants: "What shall we say, then? Shall we go on sinning so that grace may increase? By no means!" (Romans 6:1-2, NIV). The New Covenant ties are love and grace that cover and command families through difficult and even dysfunctional times.

The Old Covenant was designed to change one's behavior. Think about it. Behavior change is what the Ten Commandments are all about. Essentially, God was saying, "Watch what you do." The New Covenant takes it a step further: it's about changing one's entire being through grace.

This time, God is saying, "Watch who you are." If you follow the New Covenant, then you will still do the right things through Jesus. You will do them not because you are afraid but because you are different. Once you believe in Christ and God, the Holy Spirit will enter you, and you will have an unbroken relationship with God.

Now, you might be thinking, "Great, Bishop Dudley. Thanks for the lesson. But what does all this covenant stuff have to do with my husband zoning out, my kids taking drugs, or my wife being more concerned about Facebook than with her family?"

That is a great question.

I will give you a great answer: Everything!

God's two covenants are with and for families. God invites you to be in covenant with Him and with your family. When you embrace this covenant, your family life will change. How do you embrace this concept? Keep reading.

A fabulous family is a covenant family.

Taken together, the covenants God made with His people have five qualities that can serve you as you try to get your family heading in the right direction: grace, intentionality, intimacy, empowerment, and learning from life's lessons.

Grace

We received offers for these covenants from God not because we have done anything wonderful. Quite the contrary. As humans, we have done lots of awful things to ourselves and each other. We received these covenants because God loves us. Without exception. Without qualification. Without end. Quite simply, grace is love—unconditional love. Now, I am not talking about romantic love, although that kind of love is, of course, important. This is the love of God, who loves us when we do not deserve it. Every family needs unconditional love. No family is perfect.

We can never be God. But we can try to model ourselves after Him. The kind of love that God offers is magnificent. Too often, people see love as a feeling. And, of course, our culture sells this feeling in products, in dating services, in clothes—in almost everything.

But the love I am talking about, the love that made God give us these two covenants, is different. It is continuous caring, an offering of opportunities, a meeting of needs. This kind of love is not a biochemical rush. Feelings can change in a second. Grace does not change. Grace is a way of thinking and behaving. God gave us the world. He gave us creativity. He gave us Jesus Christ. He also gave us free will. We can choose to accept or reject this love and these covenants, but God allows us to attempt to love in the way He does. Your family cannot make it on a lie or the latest fashions.

This is the love that a covenant family needs to be fabulous!

In your covenant family, the first principle you need to apply is grace, or love. You love unconditionally, even when you do not feel like doing so. Remember, love is not a feeling. It is an unconditional valuing of another person in the same way God unconditionally loves each of us.

Is this kind of love easy to practice within your family (or any family for that matter)? Of course not.

It is easy to love your daughter when she just won the MVP on the basketball team and ranked first in her class. It is much harder to love her when she tells you that she just had unprotected sex and might be pregnant. It is easy to love your son when his football team just won the state championship and he has been offered a scholarship to a major D2 college. It is much harder to love him when you get a phone call from him from the local jail. He failed a sobriety test and is being booked for driving under the influence and drug possession. It's easy to love your husband when he brings home the bacon and provides you with a great house for the family that you have created together. It is much harder to love him when you prowl Facebook and discover he is having an affair. It is easy to love your wife when she is dressed to the nines and gives you that special smile. It's harder to love her when you discover that she has a spending problem and has just racked up twenty thousand dollars in credit card debt through binge shopping.

It is not easy to love unconditionally. But we are called to do that. We have to model ourselves after God's love. He loves us no matter what we do. In a covenant family, the members love unconditionally.

I have one word of caution. While we are called to love unconditionally, that call does not mean that God wants us to be doormats. He doesn't. God does not want us to be emotionally, spiritually, or financially abused, either. God loves unconditionally, but people do pay the price when they choose not to return the love. Nothing will contribute more to the acceleration of your family's dysfunction than failing to return this type of love or taking advantage of it. By the same token, you can unconditionally love a physically abusive partner or a drug-addicted child, but you are never called upon by God to allow yourself to be hurt by them. Don't confuse feelings with actions. You are called upon to love the thief who breaks into your home, but you should still call the police. We are called to love unconditionally, but that call does not mean people don't suffer consequences for their behavior.

Intentionality

If grace is the first quality of a covenant family, the second is intentionality. What is intentionality? Quite simply, it's a sense of direction. Going where you want to go. Knowing where you want to go. It's a compass, a roadmap.

For a Christian, the ultimate roadmap consists of working out your salvation, accepting God's grace in your life, achieving eternal life with God when you die, and discipling as many people as possible along the way. This roadmap may seem simple. And it is. But we live in a complicated world, one full of seductions, temptations, feelings of anger, greed, and lust that can run amok and send you spiraling out of control. All of the deadly sins and some of the less deadly ones, too.

Then, there are the distractions that surround us. *Who won the football game? Who won the White House? What's my Facebook feed say? I should try that new drink at the bar. That woman is attractive; a little harmless flirting never hurt. Wow, I really want that new smartphone.*

Distractions are everywhere, and we live in a culture that encourages us to succumb to our impulses: *You deserve the latest trends. You deserve to get angry and lash out. Not happy with your marriage? You deserve to be able to throw it away and find somebody else. You deserve a house you can barely afford. You deserve that new car. You deserve a perfect child, perfect mate, perfect life!*

But in reality, you deserve better than all this. And so does your family.

God's covenant with us is about intentionality, about being on point, on task. God was intentional about loving us constantly. He did not say to the Israelites, "You are My chosen people… this week…until I find somebody else." Christ did not say, "This is My new covenant with you until I decide that I'll focus on something else." God is consistent with you because He knows what He wants for you—eternal salvation. He has an endpoint in mind, and He is always gently steering you toward that goal. God is intentional!

You have to be intentional, too. You want to figure out what your family's goals are. Once you have determined your goals, you have to stick to them and make these goals the basis for your behaviors. For example, what if your daughter tells you that she has become sexually active at the age of fifteen or has gotten hooked on pain pills? Is this an occasion for you to yell and scream at her, telling her how she's throwing her life away, how she has disappointed you, how she has brought shame to your family and will never amount to anything?

It can be. But what is the goal? Isn't the goal to show unconditional love to your daughter and gently work to steer her away from potentially self-destructive behaviors? If it is strong enough, your intentionality can make you resist becoming angry. Anger might be an appropriate feeling, but will expressing it help? What's your intent? When you are intentional, every interaction with your spouse or your children becomes an occasion to forward your family's mission.

In the Old Covenant, God gave us rules. Remember, they are called the Ten Commandments, not the Ten Suggestions. They are rules and not suggestions because they help us to shape our behavior, to remember what is important and what can destroy our relationships and ourselves. In the New Covenant, Christ gave us perhaps the best rule of all to help us to be intentional: "Love your neighbor as yourself" (Mark 12:31, NIV). If we obey this rule, then we automatically obey all the others. God's laws and commandments shape our lives and our behavior.

God, of course, is always intentional. Everything on the earth has a purpose. You just have to figure out what it is. When you bring intentionality to your family, you will know where you are going, and you can shape your responses and your proactive behavior to move your family in the right direction. The end justifies the means; you intend to get to the picture you visualize for your family. When you are intentional, roadblocks are stair steps. Intentionality of love clears the path for gearing up for a fabulous family.

Intimacy

The Old Covenant between God and His people was about following the law. While families need rules to function well, they also need something else: intimacy. The New Covenant is an invitation to be intimate with Jesus Christ. This Covenant does not invite you just to worship Jesus Christ and admire Him. The New Covenant invites you to be in a relationship with Him, to invite Him into your heart, and to be intimate with Him.

What is intimacy? It is probably one of the most misused terms in the English language today. Most people, when they hear the word *intimacy*, think of sex.

That is not what intimacy is. Two people can be sexually active together and not be intimate at all. Their hearts could be closed to one another while their bodies are open to each other. Intimacy is closeness, an openness, a sharing of what is in your heart and on your mind with others, especially others you trust and are close to. Now, this call to intimacy does not mean that you let it all hang out with all your family members. Your intimacy has to be appropriate. You might share a personal problem with your spouse that you shouldn't share with a child or even a teenager because they're not your emotional equal. They're not able to reciprocate your intimacy.

What creates intimacy? Trust, interest, and vulnerability. Would you ever tell something to somebody you didn't trust? Would you turn your finances over to an advisor who seems to be in it for his own personal gain? Would you tell your personal problems to a counselor who does not quite seem to take your issues seriously? Would you give your case to a lawyer who does not seem competent? No, of course you wouldn't. So you would not give yourself to a family whose members are not intimate with each other.

If all this is true, then would you expect your spouse or child to tell you about something when they do not trust you? No, you have to create trust to have intimacy.

If trust is the first component, then interest is the second. God is interested in us. He wants us to talk to Him through prayer, worship, and gratitude. He was interested in the success of the people of Israel. He was interested enough to test Abraham, have Noah build an ark, make a covenant with Moses, and talk with Job when he did not understand what was happening to him. He was interested enough to continue His relationship with us and even send His Son to die for our sins. He listens to our prayers.

You need to be interested and cultivate a sense of interest in all family members by all the members of the family. Most importantly, just as God is, be available to your family. Pay attention to one another. Turn off the TV. Power down the computer. Put away the smartphone, and just spend time talking with your spouse, your son, your daughter. Pray together. Generally, people want to do better in their lives when others are interested and know them well.

Finally, intimacy is about vulnerability. Now, you have to be careful here. I am not telling you to go out and proclaim your deepest and darkest secrets to the whole world. That's not wise. But what I am telling you is that if others see you share parts of yourself with them, they will see you being vulnerable with them, and they will want to reciprocate. To have intimacy, you need to be vulnerable with those you love. Choose carefully.

Empowerment

A covenant family is empowered in three ways. It possesses authority, a sense of identity, and a sense of direction. A covenant family knows who it is. It celebrates and uses its strengths, and it knows and controls its weaknesses as well. Finally, a covenant family knows where it is going. It is like having a family business, and every member has a profit share. They all must know their call, assignment, and distinction to empower the family to succeed.

In Numbers 26 and 27, we learn that Moses empowered the daughters of Zelophehad: Mahlah, Noa, Hoglah, Milkah, and Tirzah. The father had died without male heirs, and his title and lands were about to be lost since his daughters possessed no right of inheritance. The daughters brought their case before Moses, who, it must be noted, was not quite sure about what to do. What Moses did do was go to God for advice. God told Moses that the women should be given shares of the land. The lesson to learn here is that the women got what they deserved because Moses took his wisdom—his empowerment as a leader of an extended family—from God.

Moses was not the first Old Testament figure to use the empowerment given to him by God to instruct the next generation. When King David was about to die, he gave his son Solomon strict advice about how to prosper as a king:

> When David was about to die, he instructed his son Solomon, "I'm about to leave this world. Be strong and mature. Fulfill your duty to the LORD your God. Obey his directions, laws, commands, rules, and written instructions as they are recorded in Moses' Teachings. Then you'll succeed in everything you do wherever you may go. You'll succeed because the LORD will keep the promise he made to me: 'If your descendants are faithful to me with all their hearts and lives, you will never fail to have an heir on the throne of Israel.'" (1 Kings 2:1-4, GW)

Both Moses and David recognized that if we do what God asks and follow His advice, justice—both in the world at large and in families—ensues.

The covenants between God and His people empowered them: "Be strong and courageous. Do not be afraid or terrified because of them, for the LORD your God goes with you; he will never leave you nor forsake you" (Deuteronomy 31:6, NIV). In the Gospel of Luke, Christ says, "I have given you authority to trample on snakes and scorpions and to overcome all the power of the enemy; nothing will harm you" (Luke 10:19, NIV). Finally, in Isaiah, God says, "So do not fear, for I am with you; do not be dismayed, for I am your God. I will strengthen you and help you; I will uphold you with my righteous right hand" (Isaiah 41:10, NIV). Believers are empowered; they don't go into battle alone; they have a powerful ally on their side.

A covenant family possesses authority. It knows that it is a group of people who belong to and with each other. A covenant family also knows that its members are special, put on earth with each other to do extraordinary things that will advance the work of God. Members of a covenant family respect each other as children of God. "Accept one another, then, just as Christ accepted you, to bring praise to God" (Romans 15:7, NIV). Now, respect and acceptance do not mean that members of a covenant family tolerate everything from each other.

Far from it.

They expect the best from each other and themselves. That they respect each other also means they respect each person's role in the family and know that God put them in those roles for a reason. There are no accidents. Spouses have to support and love each other. They have to remain faithful to each other, even when powerful forces threaten to pull them apart. Parents must instruct and, yes, discipline children. Being harsh is not called for. As Paul says in Ephesians, "Fathers, do not exasperate your children; instead, bring them up in the training and instruction of the Lord" (Ephesians 6:4, NIV). But if, as Paul recognizes, harshness isn't called for, neither is saying that anything goes. In Proverbs, we are told, "Discipline your children, for in that there is hope; do not be a willing party to their death" (Proverbs 19:18, NIV). Parents show a great deal of disrespect for their children when they do not guide them, enforce sane rules, or have high expectations for their children. God certainly has high expectations for us.

A covenant family has a sense of identity. Its members know what they stand for, know the family business, and know their values. Today, in a consumer and entertainment-based economy, many sources try to give us our identities: our work, sports teams, and characters. What movie character are we? Are we Democrats, Republicans, Greens? Are we Steelers fans? Are we liberal? Are we conservative? Are we upper middle class or lower middle class? Do we shop at Target or Walmart? Do we like Coke or Pepsi?

All these parts of one's identity are fun. Some of them are even important. But a covenant family knows that its fundamental identity does not come from a store preference, a beverage choice, or a political party affiliation. A covenant family knows that its true identity comes from God: "Before I formed you in the womb I knew you, before you were born I set you apart; I appointed you as a prophet to the nations" (Jeremiah 1:5, NIV). A family identity consists of a family's calling, a family's business or mission, and a family's purpose. As Jesus says in the Gospel of Luke, "I must be about My Father's business" (Luke 2:49, NKJV). Each family should know its identity and what it does.

This sense of identity also gives the family its values: togetherness, loyalty, love, mutual support, and integrity. These values will not come from the products we buy, the teams we watch, or even the political candidates we support. Instead, the importance of a covenant family comes from a timeless source: God and His Word. Genesis reminds us that we are creations of God: "So God created mankind in his own image, in the image of God he created them" (Genesis 1:27, NIV). Ultimately, our identity comes from Him.

The covenant family never forgets who it is and what it believes. This sense of identity helps the covenant family weather the many storms of life. If you do not know who you are and what you stand for, then you will do whatever pops into your head, whatever makes you feel good at the moment. That kind of behavior leads to no good in the long run.

When you have a strong sense of identity, certain kinds of actions are dictated. Other types are entirely off-limits because they do not fit with who you are. For a covenant family, its sense of identity is a lot like the promise of the Second Covenant. You will not do things because someone tells you what to do. Instead, you will do some things and not do other things because they either conform or do not conform to Christ's demand to love others. Colossians 3:1-2 says, "Since, then, you have been raised with Christ, set your hearts on things above, where Christ is, seated at the right hand of God. Set your minds on things above, not on earthly things" (NIV). You will do things out of natural conformity with grace. For a covenant family, who you are dictates what you do. The members of a covenant family will love and support each other; they will share with each other; they will remind each other of their mission, and they will stick to this mission. Members of a covenant family will not succumb to distractions; they will not despise or belittle each other. While they will be supportive, members of a covenant family will not negatively enable each other. Most importantly, members of a covenant family will respect each other and their roles in the family, and they will respect the covenant God has with all the family members.

Finally, a covenant family is empowered through a sense of vision. As Proverbs says, "Where there is no revelation, people cast off restraint..." (Proverbs 29:18, NIV). In other words, when people don't have a sense of what's important and where they want to go, they do almost anything—even things that damage themselves and others.

Members of a covenant family, the most fabulous kind of family, know where they want to go. On the most basic level, members of a covenant family want to go to heaven at the conclusion of a successful life. But that last phrase—*a successful life*—what does that mean?

The parents of a covenant family are responsible for teaching children what is important and what is not. To teach them what they should do and what they should not do. Some people argue that the word *should* is wrong because it implies obligation and even guilt. But you know what? Guilt isn't bad. It helps you to change direction when you need to. Guilt is the pain you feel when something hurts. You stop because you want the pain to stop.

Parents have an obligation in a covenant family to set the course of the family. What is the family about? What are its goals? Well, a covenant family, like any other, is about having a place to live, food to eat, and clothes to wear. But those are just the basics. The parents in a covenant family help to determine the larger goals: to help the children learn fundamental values and the business of the family, to figure out what they want to do with their lives, to determine how they can be of service to others, and to figure out what is right and what is wrong. All this sounds like a lot of work. And it is. But does that mean that a covenant family never has any fun? Of course not. Joy and fun are an essential part of a family and of life itself. God meant for us to have joy in our lives. But the best kind of joy comes from doing what you were meant to do, what God designed you to do. A covenant family always keeps in mind its end goals. This vision keeps it on track and helps to keep things moving smoothly.

Life Lessons

Finally, a covenant family learns from life's lessons. Bad things happen to everybody. Sometimes, like Job, we question God's wisdom or even our own. The question is not how to prevent every bad thing from happening, because bad things will happen. The question is whether the *same* bad things keep happening and whether you use them as learning tools to see what to do and what not to do. A covenant family has a history and learns from it.

In the chapters that follow, I will deal with the needs of many kinds of families and show you how you can apply covenant family principles to any situation and get your family on track to success and happiness. In each chapter, I will tell you stories from my experience as a pastor. I'll give you biblical insight into problems, and I will ask you to reflect and see how you can apply the principles of the covenant family to your family's problems.

I will include chapters relevant to a specific family structure and some that apply more generally. The most important thing to remember when reading is to internalize the five principles of a covenant family. Scan the table of contents for the chapters that address your family life and read those chapters first. The chapters that do not immediately apply to your family life will help you help other families that you are in a relationship with. The book's entirety will help families become fabulous families through covenant-based living. Every family is connected through community, so no matter your family makeup, this entire book will bless you so you can be a blessing to others.

When you have a covenant family, you have a fabulous family. Who doesn't want that?

Chapter 2

The Nuclear Family

It's not *Black-ish* anymore—if it ever was.

Even the tightest, most together nuclear family faces challenges today that were unheard of a generation ago: two working parents, kids involved in various activities, sibling rivalries, kids working, and social media. Then there are the temptations of drugs, teenage sex, and suggestive music. There is a demand for more goods: smartphones, sneakers, laptops. In addition, television shows and the internet advertise a hundred lifestyles, most of which are, biblically speaking, each more decadent than the next: *If you do not like your house, then get another. If you do not like your mate, then get another. If you do not like your gender, then get another. If you do not like the sex or eye color of your new child, then choose another.* And on and on.

A thousand arms are pulling you in a million directions.

Where does it all end?

In disaster?

Well, maybe, but it doesn't have to. The big question for you is, "Where are you going?" Most families do not have a clue beyond the next couple of days or maybe the weekend.

But if you have a covenant family, then you have a sense of direction, a vision, a road map, and a plan. And that is ninety percent of the game.

First off, you and your spouse are a team: "Two are better than one, because they have a good return for their labor: If either of them falls down, one can help the other up. But pity anyone who falls and has no one to help them up. Also, if two lie down together, they will keep warm. But how can one keep warm alone?" (Ecclesiastes 4:9-11, NIV). You're there to support each other. This support will enable both of you to face the challenges of your family.

You will have a lot of challenges. I know this because, as a husband and a father, I've faced lots of challenges in my family.

Remember, though, that no matter what challenges you face, as parents and spouses, you have the responsibility to set the tone for the family, to steer its direction beyond the obstacles. You must be proactive and not reactive. The stability depends on both of you. The gravitational pull of the two of you together keeps the children in their orbit.

The covenant family keeps you proactive and prevents you from having to put out fires constantly.

The mission, this sense of steering the direction of your family—your first ministry—must come before anything else: jobs, activities, web surfing, etc.

Why?

Because the family is a crucible. Young people are shaped and molded for their futures, both here and in heaven. Our first assignment is to lead each other and our children to God. We have to teach and live by example in God's plan for us. We can guide our kids to be lawyers, ballers, teachers, and investors, but our greatest gift—our most outstanding achievement, and what should be our only assignment—is to teach them the pathway to God and His grand plan for the family. The rest follows. This is the only way to stay close to them and the only way to ensure that they will see their way back from any challenges or issues in faith.

Remember that parenthood is a gift from God. As Psalm 127 says, "Children are a heritage from the LORD, offspring a reward from him. Like arrows in the hands of a warrior are children born in one's youth" (3-4, NIV). The psalmist ushers us into the biblical world of agrarian living and warfare. Like crops, children are gifts. In biblical terms, the more children, the more crops can be harvested and the more warriors there are for the nation's armies. But with gifts come responsibilities. If children are arrows, then it is your responsibility to aim the arrows in the right direction to hit the bullseye.

To hit that bullseye, let's apply the five elements of a covenant family—grace, intentionality, intimacy, empowerment, and learning life's lessons—to see how these elements can help you to lead your family.

Grace

Let's start at the beginning, with grace.

Grace is love. It's unearned love, unmerited divine favor, the kind that God gives each of us. God loved us and created us. Ideally, you fell in love with your spouse and wanted to create a fabulous life with that person. Obeying God's injunction to be fruitful and multiply, your love for your spouse created a child or children. More than almost anything else, love is at the core of a covenant family, a nuclear family, a fabulous family.

This love must be unconditional. God does not just love us on Sundays. He does not just love us on good days. He also loves us on bad days, on days when we have fallen short. We live in a world in which we are encouraged to have lots of conditional love: *I'll love you if you love me—if you do what I want, say what I want you to say, look like I want you to look.*

No, that's not how it works.

It should be, "I love you no matter what you do."

If you have picked your spouse carefully, then they feel the same way. This is the beginning of a covenant family.

How do we love unconditionally? First, we must be still and listen. That sounds easy, but it's not. Opening ourselves up to others unconditionally is difficult. You have to clear the decks. Put away your work. Turn off the TV. Put away the smartphone. Then just listen. You have to put away some other things as well: your preconceptions, your desire to solve problems, and your judgment; yes, your judgment of your mate, your family. You listen not only with your ears but with your eyes. You turn your body toward them to give them your undivided attention.

If you do all this and just listen to your spouse and child, then you are giving them a gift, the unconditional love that God gives you. Of course, if you are being asked for advice, then feel free to share it. But if someone asks for your attention, then you give that, just as God gives us His attention when we ask for it in prayer.

James 1:19 says, "My dear brothers and sisters, take note of this: Everyone should be quick to listen, slow to speak and slow to become angry" (NIV). Speaking and becoming angry happen very quickly. But as I know from my work as a pastor and, more importantly, in my mission as a father, listening takes time and creates trust.

Let me tell you a story from my own life that I hope will serve as an example of how to listen. My son had come home on break from college during his freshman year. One cold night after church, we began to talk about college life. We went on as fathers and sons do—talking classes, food, girls, and friends. Suddenly, he paused and looked concerned. Then my son said that he had something he really wanted to tell me. His demeanor and the change from the joking tone of the previous conversation drew my attention. I knew, in a way, what was coming—something big, something adult, something I was not sure that I was prepared for.

My mind raced to every conceivable problem. Was he homesick? Did he flunk out? Did he have girl trouble? Did he get someone pregnant? Did they have an abortion? My imagination created all sorts of hypothetical problems, each more devastating than the last. My mind raced everywhere but to the one problem that he wanted to discuss. I truly did not see it coming. Not my son. Not in my house.

He told me that he had been smoking marijuana since his senior year in high school. *What?! Since high school?! I am a pastor. Where did this problem come from?* I tried to stay calm. I wanted to put it in perspective. Smoking pot is not the end of the world. It's a problem for many teenagers—not ideal, but not abnormal. But to not know or even have an idea that it was happening?

Wow. More than I could take.

I was devastated. We never knew. He was a model son in so many ways—involved with youth ministries and school extracurricular activities. I felt that he had always been honest with me. This seemed like a betrayal. It felt like a confessional. I had to be both father and preacher. Although I did not say anything, I went straight to how this disclosure made me feel. I looked right past the fact that he shared with me and seemed to want advice—a reaction, anything—from his dad. I could not speak, though. I could not even think.

What was I supposed to say?

He finally broke the silence and said that he felt like he had to be honest with me. He told me that he had stopped smoking it, but even so, he wanted me to know about it because we had always had a great relationship, and he could not keep something this big from me any longer.

I thanked him for that, and to my best recollection, I asked him to share more. I didn't interrogate him, although I wanted to. Instead, I just asked about his feelings and his decision to stop. I told him how proud I was that he stopped and that he had told me. I also told him that he needed to use this as an example of how to handle other difficult challenges in his future, and he agreed. We needed always to share—father to son—man to man.

Later, my son disclosed to me that he thought I would snap, but I didn't. I felt like if I had done so, if I would have even said what I was thinking at that moment, then he would have never shared again. I did not want to pass judgment, but instead, I wanted to build on this moment that he had created—a moment in which he could share with me about anything else in his life. It was not easy for either of us.

But here is the point.

Even though I wanted to speak, maybe even to preach and judge, I didn't. I could have opened fire with a litany of accusations and condemnations. But what was my job as a father? Beyond "straightening out" my son, above all others, my job was to love him unconditionally, no matter what he told me.

Was it easy to do that job? Not at all. I had to overcome my natural impulses of teaching and preaching. While those are good impulses, and sometimes very necessary, unconditionally loving him by unconditionally listening to him was what was needed. The results were outstanding. He felt empowered to tell me anything. Our relationship could have exploded or withered and died or become shallow if I had verbally attacked him for smoking pot. Instead, because I listened, our relationship blossomed.

Isn't that what you want? Try unconditional love and listening with your spouse and children. God listens to you. Try listening to someone you love.

Intentionality

So, let's say you're at the wheel of a ship. Someone says, "Turn left." You turn left. Someone else shouts, "Turn right." You turn right. A third person says, "Go full reverse." You shrug your shoulders and back up. Do you think the ship is going to go anywhere if you steer like this?

It isn't.

A ship's captain sets his course and sails his ship toward his destination. Sure, he might steer around a storm, but he keeps going until he sets his sights on the shore. A good captain does not just meander around the ocean. He is deliberate, and he knows where he is going.

In other words, a good captain is intentional. God is intentional. God intended on making us the way He did in our mother's womb. God's identity is seen throughout creation. God is not random, nor does He want our family life to be random.

You and your spouse need to be intentional as well. You cannot sail the ship in circles and expect to get anywhere. So, what does it mean to be intentional in a covenant family?

First, you have to discern your family's assignment, the thing that God put you on earth to do. The way you know your family's assignment is by looking at what your family as a whole does for a living.

For example, if dad is a firefighter and mom is a nurse, then your family assignment is helping people.

Some families are good with the law. Others are entrepreneurial. Some are into science and medicine, others the arts. Every family has a calling. God has assigned every family something to do on the earth. If a family can find a true calling and build the finances, the beliefs, the traditions, and more on that premise, then no matter the challenges that come their way, they will sustain the family life that they all buy into.

A couple of questions might be popping into your head right now. First, you might be saying to yourself, "Bishop, my wife is a flower designer, and I'm a chiropractor. We don't have a business or a mission that unifies us."

Actually, you probably do. Drill down into your jobs and see what the core functions or values of the jobs are. Since you and your spouse selected each other based, I hope, on shared values, your jobs probably reflect these values. Those values can serve as guideposts for your family. If one of you is a cop and the other a paralegal, then your values probably revolve around helping people seek justice.

The next question you might ask is how those values help you to be intentional as a family. It's a good question. The answer is that they are critical.

For example, if you and your husband are about justice, then that value can help steer your family. If your son is bullying someone or your daughter is taking advantage of a friend, then you can say to them, "Hey, we're about justice in this family. It's what we do." You can insist your son apologize and your daughter repay her friend. These values can steer your family. God gave you these values. Use them.

Second, you need to establish your voice and belief system, hold it to your heart, and offer it to God. You must make it very clear that this belief system is the way of the household for all members. If you do this, the vision of the family is clear and unified.

Third, you have to develop the family on all levels—give credence to the beliefs and needs of the children and the parents alike.

Notice how in Deuteronomy 6:5-9 Moses told the families to ensure their assignment just before they entered the Promised Land:

> Love the LORD your God with all your heart and with all your soul and with all your strength. These commandments that I give you today are to be on your hearts. Impress them on your children. Talk about them when you sit at home and when you walk along the road, when you lie down and when you get up. Tie them as symbols on your hands and bind them on your foreheads. Write them on the doorframes of your houses and on your gates. (NIV)

The Dudley family assignment is to help and nurture people spiritually. All of us are called to the ministry in some aspect. Our family vision statement is to change a life in our lifetime.

A covenant family honors the gifts, talents, and souls of all its members, including both the children and the often-overworked parents. People need time to develop their abilities. You need to take your son to football practice or your daughter to cheerleading. What might not be so obvious is that you need to give your wife time to go running, or your husband time to do some woodworking or painting. And you all need time to pray and reflect.

Covenant families are intentional in how they budget their time. Do you just spend your evenings zoning out, or do you spend some time helping your children develop themselves and sometimes developing yourself as well?

Intimacy

Family is where we all learn the fundamentals of relationships. In fact, in life, if you are having any trouble managing relationships at all—with a girlfriend, boyfriend, co-worker, or even God—it is probably because you learned the wrong way to handle intimacy because of some dynamics in your own family. I always say that everyone comes from somebody's family unit—from presidents, heads of state, and millionaires to mass murderers, rapists, and gang bangers. The homeless had a family at one time. The addicts and other people suffering in our society had a family—maybe still have a family. In that family, they learned how to have relationships.

The covenant family should be an incubator for intimacy. Let's remember the three components of intimacy: trust, interest, and vulnerability. The covenant family helps to produce an environment in which all three of these qualities can flourish.

Do you spend time together, maybe watching a movie, or even praying or talking? You can give your family a lot of things: a house, money, vacations, education. But perhaps the most important thing you can give them is yourself—intimacy. Spend time with them. Pray with them. Play with them. Talk with them. These things are not extras. They are essentials.

For a covenant family, play and prayer can be combined.

For example, my wife Glenda and I talked about Jesus to our children. Before I was a full-time pastor or chaplain in the Air Force, faith was a topic of family conversation. We talked about it over dinner, watching TV, or just sitting around playing our favorite board game, Trouble.

These were never forced conversations. They were just always part of the fabric of our lives. Friday was family night for us. So, of course, Jesus and our faith were a part of the night. For example, before we would make a pizza and watch a movie—our favorite Friday night activity—we watched a cartoon episode about the Bible. We also prayed before the movie started—part of the routine. This routine led us to my children's questions about Jesus and their faith. These Jesus-and-pizza sessions helped us bring my daughter to Christ at age ten and my son to Christ at age nine. I was honored to baptize both of them.

We just made God a regular natural part of our lives.

In addition to having special nights with your family where you share, you can turn every night, every dinner, into an occasion for intimacy.

In my own home, I always encouraged many activities like sports, academic clubs, outreach with the church, and more—whatever my wife and I thought would make our children more well-rounded, happier, and more successful. As a result, dinnertime became an interesting concept in our house.

We always turned the TV off at dinner. I always asked, what did you learn today in school? I asked them "what" questions, not "why" questions. What made you feel that, do that, think that? "What" questions require intentional, thoughtful responses. My kids hated those sorts of questions and would say: "Daddy, you always ask hard questions." But these questions made our family more intimate. The older our family got, the easier it got. It became so easy that my son called a family meeting while we were on vacation. He asked all of us to describe each other. One good thing—a description and how we felt about each other. He was a junior in college by then. I believe this came as a result of the culture of intimacy that was created at the dinner table.

It is intimate moments like these that we treasure for the rest of our lives. These intimate moments also serve as a school to educate your children about being in a relationship with others.

You may be providing your family with a great house, a cool car, lavish vacations, and first-rate education. But if you are not providing your children with intimacy, then you are making them poor.

We are intimate with our families because we love them. We love them because God loved us. Like 1 John 4:19 says, "We love because he first loved us" (NIV).

The scripture here tells us that God has loved us, and as a result, we love others. By bringing His Word and His plan for us into our homes and teaching our children what that means to the family, we show that love for others is the way to go. We are also reiterating that God's love for us is endless, and His plan is in place, no matter what. Adhering to our Christian principles can help to guide us in times of doubt when it seems that the world is against us or the universe is sending us mixed messages.

Empowerment

We live in an age in which people say, "It takes a village to raise a child."

Really?

How well has that concept worked?

Children who grow up outside of a nuclear family or do not spend much time with their parents run all sorts of risks: teen pregnancies, drug addiction, increased chances of suicide, gang involvement.

The Bible is very clear that the responsibility for taking care of people, especially children, resides with the family: "Anyone who does not provide for their relatives, and especially for their own household, has denied the faith and is worse than an unbeliever" (1 Timothy 5:8, NIV). This passage suggests that it does not take a village; it takes a family. If you count on the village to do the work you should be doing, then your faith is not very strong.

While I understand that sometimes an intact nuclear family is not possible, I firmly believe that in addition to it taking a village to raise a child, it takes a family—a covenant family.

Study after study says that an intact, functional nuclear family is one of the best predictors of children's success.

A covenant family is an empowered family because it possesses authority, identity, and vision. The village worked when the values of the village were mutual. Now village values are contaminated and offer limited help. What empowerment would that child receive?

In terms of raising children, we need more covenant families and fewer villages.

The family needs to be a functioning community of its own. With authority given to us by God, we manage our households. With the identity and vision that only a family can offer, we impart wisdom to our children.

Who can we blame when our kids go astray? Who can we turn to when our family members seem to be in spiritual distress? Who is ultimately responsible for all that affects our lives? We are.

That responsibility may seem overwhelming, but if you are part of a covenant family, then you are empowered. You have the authority of God. You also have a sense of vision and identity that helps you keep your family on the right path.

Don't give up control to the village.

Learning from Life's Lessons

You have to know what you believe, and you have to be unafraid of teaching what you believe to your children.

Nowadays, some parents say, "I won't teach any beliefs, and I'll let the kids work them out on their own when they become adults. I won't make them go to church because I never liked it when I was made to go to church. I won't make them do this or that. I will let them develop via their own choices." That is a recipe for disaster.

The Bible recognizes that children must be taught proper values. Proverbs tells us: "Start children off on the way they should go, and even when they are old they will not turn from it" (22:6, NIV). In the First Book of Timothy, we are told, "That is why we labor and strive, because we have put our hope in the living God, who is the Savior of all people, and especially of those who believe. Command and teach these things" (1 Timothy 4:10-11, NIV).

You have to teach your children values, and you have to discipline your children when they depart from these values to learn from their experiences. Unless you're a sadist, no discipline is harsher than what life will provide for your children, so it is best if children learn lessons and experience discipline from somebody who cares about them. That's you. In Proverbs, it says, "Discipline your children, and they will give you peace; they will bring you the delights you desire" (29:17). Of course, what discipline means is up to you, but you are not being intentional if you allow "anything goes" behavior. If you do allow anything, then that is what you will get. You do not want just any outcome for your family.

When you think about discipline, the concepts of priorities and boundaries should be kept in mind. Priorities and boundaries are really just mirror opposites. Priorities tell you what you should do, and boundaries tell you what you should not do.

The first thing that we must do is understand what a priority is and what it is not. Some things in our lives are not necessary, but society has told us that we need them. How stylish do we need to be? How aggressive do we need to be? How smart do we need to be? Society tells us that we should always be on the lookout for the most up-to-date fashion, the best-looking person, the next chance to prove ourselves tougher than the next person. How much do our children need these things or experiences? We need to do society one better. We need to determine what the necessary values, beliefs, and activities are for our children.

Also, we must learn how to say no to some things that our children want to do and realize that saying no is okay. We must never feel that we have to be everywhere and do everything. Let's learn the ministry of "No!" which is just another word for a boundary.

What is a good way to determine discipline for kids? Priorities and boundaries. Does a child's behavior interfere with the child's ability to accomplish a priority? For example, premarital sex might interfere with the child's college attendance. A baby out of wedlock will slow the road to success. "Exceptions" are easy to point to, but the data tells us the "rule." Drinking could interfere with schoolwork. Cell phones might place a drain on a family's financial resources. In addition, a covenant family has to concern itself with spiritual priorities as well. Does a particular behavior, while seemingly okay, interfere with a child's spiritual growth? If it does, set a boundary.

How?

One thing you can do when a child gets into some trouble is sit down with that child and talk about what the family has decided is important. Then ask the child whether the behavior will help get him or her closer to what is important. If the child sees that the behavior will not get him closer to what he thinks is important, then the child is more likely to develop a boundary.

Priorities and boundaries: the core of discipline and a way to learn from life's lessons.

Reflection Questions:

1. How does your parenting style help to mold your children?
2. How grateful are you for the gift of parenthood? What could you do to increase your gratitude?
3. Are your kids heading in the right direction? If they are not, then how do you think you could steer them in a new direction?
4. When was the last time you gave unconditional love?
5. What can you do to become a better listener for your spouse and your children?
6. What is your family's assignment? How can you use the values associated with your family's assignment to guide your family?
7. Does everybody in your family have time to develop their gifts and abilities?
8. Take some time and write out your family's belief system. What values does it embrace? What is your family all about? What is your family vision statement? Is it posted?
9. What special activities can you think of that would help you to develop intimacy with your family?
10. How good are you at saying "no"? How do you think you could become better?

Chapter 3

Single Parents

Traditionally, when we thought of families, we used to think of Mom, Dad, and the kids.

But you know what?

The world has changed in the last forty years.

According to the American Psychological Association, divorce rates are around forty to fifty percent for first marriages and are even higher for second marriages (2018). Beyond these grim numbers is another one: the National Review notes that about forty percent of all births occur out of wedlock today (2013).

So, the reality is that single parents will head many families. Now, most commonly, the custodial parent is female. However, more men are beginning to take on the role of caregiver-in-chief.

I am not saying that all traditional nuclear families were or are happy. Nevertheless, the reality is that the traditional nuclear family allows for teamwork, a division of labor, and, in the best cases, friendship and fellowship with a spouse. Those benefits are simply not present in single-parent households. You take on a lot of responsibility when you are a single parent. As the old commercial goes, you have to bring home the bacon and fry it up in a pan too.

The challenge may sound daunting, but the covenant family's principles can help you survive and prosper as a single parent. In this chapter, I will talk about how to apply the covenant family principles when you are on your own. I will also introduce you to two remarkable single parents: Dave, a single dad, and Joanna, a single mom. These two folks have a lot on their plates. Still, they live with a sense of purpose—a sense of mission—mainly because they observe the principles of the covenant family: grace, intentionality, empowerment, intimacy, and learning from life's lessons.

Before I introduce you to Dave and Joanna, let me introduce you to the strongest single parent there ever was: Mary, the mother of Christ.

Although Mary, like many single parents, felt alone and scared at times, God was on her side. In Luke 1:30, an angel tells the mother of Christ, "Do not be afraid, Mary; you have found favor with God" (NIV).

While you are not the parent of Jesus Christ, God is with you as well. Never forget that.

Mary is a perfect example of a single parent having to shoulder the burden of raising a house full of children alone. Scripture did not record when Joseph died, but we know that Mary became a single parent. Evidently, right after Jesus turned twelve or thirteen, Joseph died. We see the last reference to Joseph when they left Jesus at the temple when He was twelve. Jesus had siblings, and Mary's hands were full with a teenage Jesus, who had extraordinary skills (a gifted child if ever there was one) and siblings who did not believe in these abilities and possibly were jealous. She managed to raise a savior, the Savior, by God's grace.

With God's grace and your faith in Him, you can raise a fine child as well.

While he does not face the same challenges Mary did raising Jesus, Dave is a single dad raising an eleven-year-old daughter on his own—not an easy task when working a full-time job. He has put his daughter at the center of his life, as a good dad should. Joanna is a single mom who works at a bank to support her two sons. These two single parents face problems, but they keep their covenant with their children at the center of their lives. This covenant separates these two single parents from millions of others in similar situations.

Even if you are not a single parent, this chapter can be helpful to you because it is going to focus sharply—specifically in the intentionality section—on an issue that all parents have to deal with: children's social media use.

Grace

When asked about the role of grace in his family, Dave is incredibly candid:

> Grace in my family is really simple. We follow God's Word. God has blessed us tremendously. A few years ago, I accepted a job to go overseas for a year or two. I was excited but a little down, too, because I would be away from my daughter for two years. My daughter was absolutely against me going. I tried to explain to her that my going would enable us to quickly clear up some debt and to be able to purchase a home. She said she did not care about a house; she just wanted me there. I had already made up my mind that I was going. I had prayed about it. I wasn't sure I had received an answer from God, but I decided I was going to accept the job.

> Long story short, I got the job, but the day before I was to fly out, I got a call saying they had decided to not hire me for medical reasons that they had previously said were not a problem. I was upset, of course. I called my daughter to tell her that I lost the job. She started crying and said: "Daddy, I'm sorry." I asked her why, and she said: "Daddy, I prayed every day to God that He would not let you go on that job. I don't care about the house and extra money, but I knew you did so I asked God to get you a better job here."

Dave says that he laughed a little bit and said, "Ok, baby. No problem."

The point here is clear. As it says in 1 John 5:14, "This is the confidence we have in approaching God: that if we ask anything according to his will, he hears us" (NIV). God heard both Dave and his daughter. They both had faith that things would work out for the best. They were both right. Dave stayed home, and in less than six months, he was promoted at his current job.

You have to refer all-important decisions to God. Now, this principle may seem straightforward, and it is. However, when you are a single parent, you do not have an earthly partner. So, praying becomes more important because God is the go-to person when there is nobody else.

Dave says of this experience, "I wasn't sure I had received an answer from God to my prayers about whether or not to accept the overseas job. Honestly, I never felt right about going or accepting the job, but I made up my mind that I was going. Although I didn't hear an answer, I believe my daughter did and her prayers were answered."

So were Dave's.

Faith in God is a bedrock for all parents, but especially for single parents. In 1945, an American war movie was released called *God Is My Copilot*. As a former Air Force chaplain, I can certainly agree with the sentiments of the title of this film. When you are flying alone, as single parents do, God is your copilot, your navigator, your engineer, and your tail gunner.

Rely on Him through prayer and scripture. He will get you through the turbulence.

Joanna agrees with Dave about faith being essential.

She says that her faith keeps her strong. "Being a single parent is not easy," she says. "God is a foundation. You need God, and you're nothing without Him. There are times when you don't know how you're going to pay the power bill." Now, Joanna recognizes that God is not an ATM. You cannot call the power company and say you will pay with a scripture this month. That check would bounce.

However, as it says in Philippians 4:19, "But my God shall supply all your need according to his riches in glory by Christ Jesus" (KJV). Faith can help you through difficult times. As Luke 12:24 tells us, "Consider the ravens: for they neither sow nor reap; which neither have storehouse nor barn; and God feedeth them: how much more are ye better than the fowls?" (KJV). This scripture describes the order of creation. Birds are lower than man, the crown of God's creation. So, if He takes care of the birds, then He will certainly take care of a single-parent household. Faith makes us better than the fowls. Our needs will be provided for through our faith. God is not going to send you one hundred dollars from heaven. But if you have faith, then you might find someone who can help. Faith keeps the door to help open.

As a parent, you will find that there are moments when you will most certainly need help. Joanna says it can get tough as a single parent. There are times when she has to shut herself in her room and have what she calls a "mini-breakdown." She does not want her boys to see it because they need to have their childhoods. She knows, though, that her oldest son can tell when something is wrong—a good, responsible son, who has offered to help with bills whenever he can.

Faith in God doesn't give you an easy path as a single parent, but it does give you a path on which you can travel toward hope and love. As it says in Proverbs 14:26, "Whoever fears the LORD has a secure fortress, and for their children it will be a refuge" (NIV).

Intentionality

In this section, I will deal extensively with television and social media use. This is an area in which all parents in all kinds of families could definitely use an improvement. Kids today spend four to six hours a night on television or the internet. One question we may have is, what are these kids learning while watching the tube or surfing the web? The other question is, what else could they be doing with their time?

Now, social media is a challenge for all families. No matter your family status, not being intentional about your kids' television and social media use can be destructive. Oddly enough though, there is a correlation between low-income households and higher hours spent on social media, television, and the internet. Allowing your children almost unlimited access to media may seem like an excellent alternative to letting kids run wild outside—one that keeps them engaged and safe. The truth, though, is that social media can become a false god in your children's lives, a god that offers values that are different from those of the covenant family.

Social media use is even more of a challenge for single-parent families. The reality is that you are on your own. If you are with a partner and need some downtime, then your partner can play with the kids, take them out, or hang out with them. As a single parent, you do not have that luxury. When you are taking time out, no one's picking up the slack. This fact means that it is tempting for you to use television and social media as a kind of partner in parenting. That solution probably is not going to work very well. What type of partner would you be getting?

Unsupervised social media use can lead you to some horrible places.

Think about it. Do the founders of Google, Twitter, and Facebook share your values? Do the producers of *The Simpsons* or *The Real Housewives of Atlanta* have a covenant with your children? What about MTV, VH1, or other reality television? I do not have to tell you the answer to these questions.

Whatever your parental status, but especially if you are a single parent, then you have to be intentional in terms of your children's television and social media use. Certainly, television and social media can open worlds to you and your children. But some of these worlds are hostile to you, your values, and your children's integrity.

We live in a time of extreme capitalism—a culture that advocates for money and fame with no substance, as evidenced by the many reality shows that showcase the rich and vapid. The culture also promotes social media selfies and showing off our vacations, new clothing, and promotions at work to all our followers on Instagram and Facebook. But a "like" on our Facebook page will not make us like our dysfunction nor guide us to our family destiny.

Social media has caused us to become button pushers and mediated communicators, so people as a whole no longer build strong relationships. Thus, there is a growing void. I suggest that we get back to the days of talking to one another face-to-face and understand that we need each other.

In my family, we do not watch television when we eat dinner. When my kids were growing up, we made sure we ate at least one meal per week together—most often on Sundays. The kids were not allowed to have televisions in their rooms. We watched television together and discussed what we observed. We took the phone when they disobeyed. I even took my son's clothes when his grades dropped. He had to wear old out-of-style clothes so that I could get his attention. We took his car and made him ride the bus when he did not comply with the rules of the house.

The point is, you have to control the media and social media in the life of your family. You do not let the media control your lives.

Social media can help us—both kids and adults—maintain relationships. But social media is also a bit of never-never land. There are two kinds of social media relationships. There are the kinds that are about preserving friendships that you make in the real world. For example, kids in college can stay in touch with their high school friends and family. This kind of social media use is fantastic, but there is another kind as well: social media relationships with people you do not know. This kind of social media use can be disorienting, giving a false picture of people you think you know but really don't.

This disorientation is tough for Generation X and Baby Boomer parents who grew up before Facebook and other social media. Think what it is like for kids and young adults who have never known a world without Facebook, Twitter, or Instagram. It is easy for kids to think that what is selectively revealed about someone on Facebook discloses the whole truth about them. A long time ago, the writer Charles Dickens made the point that writing is reduction. It is not the total truth. Words are attempting to describe truth—social media is the same. No piece of writing—except for the Word, of course—can ever capture the whole truth. That maxim applies even more strongly to social media sites. Kids can enjoy these sites, but do not let the sites become your kids' reality. Consider having time reserved for social media use and be thinking about how much access to technology, such as smartphones, tablets, and internet sites, your kids need.

Because social media use can present a false picture of a person, parents need to be intentional in two ways regarding their children's use of social media. First, parents need to ensure that kids understand that what they see about a person online might not be the whole truth or even remotely close to the truth. As Ronald Reagan used to say about the Soviet Union, "Trust, but verify." I might even say not to trust very much of what you see on social media unless you know the person. Second, parents need to make sure that their children are not engaging in the same kind of persona creation and creating a false sense of who they are.

Joanna says that her oldest son is on social media all the time. She says, "There's good and bad about it. You can find out about your friends, and you can also keep up with your friends. But the key to remember is that some people live out facades on social media."

Joanna also tells her sons that they must remember that what they post on the internet is out there forever. Her older son is an entrepreneur, and social media has helped him with his business endeavors. The downside, though, is that he likes posting pictures of himself with his shirt off. Joanna tells him: "You're selling yourself. Do you want yourself on social media like that? Are you comfortable with having something you said or posted out there forever?"

One of the keys here is being aware of what your children are doing, what they are watching and seeing in the media. Joanna says that even though she's very busy—sometimes working two jobs—she has always prioritized family time. She also works to make sure her boys stay active and are not just watching television or surfing the net. To help the boys stay on track, Joanna brings them to church, where they learn scripture that can serve as a tool for them. Joanna's children also read scripture at home with her.

Dave has also found problems, not so much with social media, but with television. Dave's biggest challenge is when his daughter stays with her mom and sisters. They allow things he does not permit in his home. "She has older sisters, and they will watch shows or listen to certain music, shows like *Basketball Wives* and *The Real Housewives of Atlanta*," he says. Dave does not think that these shows are suitable for teenage girls to watch. I agree with him wholeheartedly.

The real problem with media in children's lives is that these entertainment sources can offer false gods, ones with which the real God has to compete. Television and social media provide skewed views of the world.

Not everybody is wealthy.

Not everybody is beautiful.

Not everybody is wildly successful.

In 1 Samuel 7:3-4, we are told, "Then Samuel spoke to all the house of Israel, saying, 'If you return to the LORD with all your hearts, then put away the foreign gods and the Ashtoreths from among you, and prepare your hearts for the LORD, and serve Him only; and He will deliver you from the hand of the Philistines.' So the children of Israel put away the Baals and the Ashtoreths, and served the LORD only" (NKJV).

Entertainment media and social media offer an idealized and often outrageous view of what life should be like. This view is not the Christian view, which argues that life should be about faith, work, charity, and family.

Social media is not the only area in which Dave and Joanna have learned to be intentional. Dave is very clear about spending time with his daughter. Not only does Dave enjoy his time with Joanna, but he is also open about the fact that there is another reason he hangs out with her so much. "I talk to her all the time. I spend as much time with her as possible so she can see through me and my actions what a man is supposed to be," he says. Our first experience of the opposite gender comes through our opposite-sex parent. If that relationship is not strong and healthy, it is unlikely that the child will have good bonding patterns.

Joanna is intentional about another issue that unfortunately is all too real today, especially for African American boys:

racism. Despite claims to the contrary, racism exists. Joanna wants her boys "to be aware of the existence of racism and not to be gullible and naïve." On the flip side, she does not want her boys to be overwhelmed and suspicious of everybody. Although Joanna knows that most people are not racist and does not want her sons walking on eggshells, she desires her sons to be aware of and wise about race relations in the United States.

That sounds wise to me. Although it doesn't address race specifically, Deuteronomy does deal with not forgetting the past: "But watch out! Be careful never to forget what you yourself have seen. Do not let these memories escape from your mind as long as you live! And be sure to pass them on to your children and grandchildren" (4:9, NLT). Don't be overwhelmed by the past, but don't forget it, either.

Empowerment

Empowerment is crucial for single parents simply because they do not have the tactical and strategic empowerment that even the worst of spouses can provide. Empowerment for single parents can come from many sources, even from memories of hurt or lack. As a single parent, you must find as many sources of empowerment as you can. You are simply going to need them to get through life. You may be on your own, but do not become isolated. If you do, then that can be when actual problems start: despair, depression, dysfunction.

One of Dave's primary sources of empowerment was the hurt he experienced from his biological father. Although Dave's biological father did not live with Dave and his mother, Dave saw his dad every day as a child but didn't know he was his dad. When Dave would see him in the mornings on his way to school, his father would stop him and give him fifty cents or a dollar.

"One day, by accident, I found out he was my biological dad. I was happy. He was, at the time, the most popular guy in our town," he says. Unfortunately, Dave's father dropped out of Dave's life as quickly as he had popped into it: "There were no more fifty cents or dollars." Dave says that one of his childhood longings, which was never satisfied, was to have his father come to his sporting events: "I played soccer, basketball, baseball, football, and some other sports. He has never seen me play in or coach any of the sports I've participated in to this day. He has yet to even see his granddaughter play."

This hurt has given Dave a kind of "not on my watch" attitude, one that keeps him connected to his daughter and in her life. "I'm not bitter about him not seeing me play or coach, but that is always there in my head: I will not be like that," he says. It's this source of empowerment that made Dave feel like he would be a good dad.

Clearly, you can use your own childhood experience—whether good or bad—as a tool of empowerment to guide you in what to do for your children and how to be with them. Even hurt can be empowering.

If Dave's earthly father gave him a sense of what *not* to do, then Dave's heavenly Father gave him a sense of what *to* do. Proverbs 22:6 says, "Start children off on the way they should go, and even when they are old they will not turn from it" (NIV). Dave takes very seriously the job of raising his daughter because he knows she will see how the world should treat her through him. "Through me she will learn how men should treat her because she sees how I treat her mother even though her mom and I are not together," he says.

Dave is right. Parents are role models both in terms of how kids will treat others and will expect to be treated.

One piece of advice that I would give to single parents is the same advice that I might give to someone about investing: diversify your kinds of support. Rely on God for your heavenly support, but do not get isolated and dependent only on yourself. You need other streams of support.

Joanna is a firm believer in this advice. Like Dave, Joanna knows that God is her copilot in the often-turbulent environment of single parenthood. Joanna says that besides God, her empowerment comes from several sources.

Joanna's mother and stepfather provide moral support. In times of trouble, if Joanna gets herself into a bind, then they can help financially. While Joanna likes to be independent, she is grateful that her mom and stepdad are there for her.

In addition, Joanna feels empowered by her friendships. Occasionally, she has a girls' night out or a lunch with her friends. Together, the ladies can brainstorm and share about issues that they face. Friendships are crucial for single parents. A simple phone call or a coffee or a Coke meeting can chase away the sense of isolation that even the best of single parents can feel.

Now, when you are talking about finding empowerment for your single-parent family, you of course have to find empowerment in terms of the things you cannot provide. Despite the presence of the post-modern social constructivists who argue that gender is entirely social—one of the things it is difficult, if not impossible, to do as a single parent is to provide the kind of guidance that your opposite-gender partner would. If you are a single mom, then you are not male. If you are a single dad, then you are not female. Each gender does provide something unique to children. Kids need both. So, it is vital to provide your child with guidance from someone from your opposite gender. The church or other community agencies like Big Brother/Big Sister or CARES can help.

For Joanna, another source of empowerment, especially regarding her oldest son, is her boyfriend, who will meet Joanna's son for guy time over breakfast or lunch. Having this kind of support from a relationship partner who understands what you're going through can also help dispel isolation and loneliness. For female single parents of boys, a male partner can also help provide what teenage boys desperately need: a solid male role model and camaraderie with an older male who knows the ropes and isn't afraid to show a boy how to climb them.

Finally, Joanna says that her church has empowered her. One of the churchmen, Bill, helped to serve as a role model for her oldest son. But the ladies at church also empower Joanna. They check to see how she is doing. They encourage her boys to do well in their activities and school. Joanna notes, thankfully, that they will occasionally slide her grocery money when she needs it.

Although she is a single parent, Joanna recognizes that she cannot do it alone. She needs to be empowered through her faith, her family, her friends, and the church.

Intimacy

Creating intimacy with your family is difficult enough when there are two of you to split the workload. Paradoxically, intimacy is even harder to achieve when you do not have a spouse or partner, making intimacy with your family even more critical.

I have always found that a great way to create intimacy with my family is to share meals together as often as possible. We start with a prayer, and then we open conversation, discussing what is going on in our lives. We make it open to take turns sharing while the rest of the family listens. Not only does this open the lines of communication, but it also creates a bond of trust. Dave has made it a point to practice this behavior with his daughter, even rearranging his day so he can surprise her at school or summer camp for lunch. He loves it, she loves it, and they have grown together because of it. Children can sometimes foster a lot of hatred toward a single parent, but this small act helps quell those negative feelings. Dave's actions—and yours, if you participate in this small gesture—let his daughter know beyond a shadow of a doubt that he loves her and is there for her.

Joanna echoes the sentiments of Dave by saying that she makes sure that she tells her kids every day that she loves them and wants only the best for them. They know that she would go to the ends of the earth for them. This knowledge of Joanna's love will no doubt pay off for the boys as they mature and reach manhood. Joanna's consistency of love will help her boys to develop their own consistent and loving relationships.

Joanna has hit on something important. Kids know that a parent loves them in three ways. First, the parent is simply there. Second, the parent does things for them. Third, the parent tells the kids of their love for them. This final way of showing love may seem unimportant, but it's crucial. Kids need to hear that you love them. Hearing your love proclaimed is especially important for kids in single-parent families where the other parent might not be there, might not do things for the kids, and, frankly, might not even love them.

Learning from Life's Lessons

Both Dave and Joanna have learned a lot as single parents and have a lot of wisdom to pass along to others in their situations. I encourage you to learn from them.

Dave says that he has learned a lot about partner selection. Dave says, "What's funny or a big misunderstanding to me is that there have been women that I've dated who have told me that I spend too much time with my daughter and give her too much attention. I have never understood that because most of these women are mothers. Some have broken up or stopped dating me because of the time I spend with my daughter. Now, it wasn't like I wasn't spending time with them, because I was."

Let's face it. Dating when you have a child is not easy. It is difficult for one specific reason. Your partner, and perhaps reasonably so, expects to be the priority in your life. The simple truth is that they cannot prioritize your life because you have a covenant with your child. You have to honor that covenant. One sobering fact to keep in mind is that, according to the Fourth National Incidence Study of Child Abuse and Neglect (2005-2006), while child abuse in general is decreasing in the United States, child abuse, especially in the endangerment category, actually has increased by fifty-eight percent in single-parent families.

Psychology Today reports the following: "One fact that is clear across the board: perpetrators of child abuse and neglect are most often the child's own parents. According to

NCANDS, a 2005 study showed that 79.4% of child abusers were the parents, and the next largest pool of abusers consisted of unmarried partners of the parents of child victims. A whopping 40% of child victims were abused by their mothers acting alone, and a disturbing 17.3% were abused by both parents" (2011).

It is easy to neglect children when you are working two jobs to pay the bills and nobody else is around to help. It is even easier to trust a partner you care about. But the reality is that when you are a single parent, you have to be extra vigilant, both with your actions and those of any romantic partner you have. When you have a child, you have to screen potential dating partners very carefully. You need to be honest with your potential partner about your responsibilities. Your child has to come first in any future relationship you get into. This fact will limit or perhaps even eliminate most potential dating partners.

Like it or not, this situation may help you to grow and become fully capable of loving. As it says in 1 Corinthians 13:4-8, "Love is patient, love is kind. It does not envy, it does not boast, it is not proud. It does not dishonor others, it is not self-seeking, it is not easily angered, it keeps no record of wrongs. Love does not delight in evil but rejoices with the truth. It always protects, always trusts, always hopes, always perseveres. Love never fails" (NIV).

If you ally yourself with God, then being a single parent can make you more patient, more loving, and even more selective in your future partners.

Dave has also learned something else about love. Men are conditioned from childhood to be providers and protectors. While these functions—coming out of our biology and our sociology—are normal, sometimes men forget that the best thing you can provide to your child or partner is presence, not presents. "One of the biggest things I've learned from my daughter is that spending time with her is more valuable or just as valuable as buying her things," he explains. Dave has hit on something significant here. Of course, you want to provide everything for your child. This desire may be especially true if you are a single parent. Be careful, though. Don't try to buy your child's love. Your children may say that they want the latest clothes or the newest game. Usually, though, what children want is your love and attention.

As Dave says, give the gift of yourself to your children. "That is the advice I would give not just to single fathers but to fathers, period. Spend time with your children."

Of course, there are problems even when you do spend time with your kids. Dave says, "I referee sports part-time. I also coach youth sports. One of my dreams has always been to be able to coach my own children. My daughter has recently gotten into sports. I love it. But there is one thing that I've had to get over. She absolutely does not want me to coach her."

Completely crestfallen by his daughter not wanting him as her coach, Dave says that he recognizes that children will often take criticism from other adults better than from their own parents. For example, when Dave asked his daughter why she would be okay with being "yelled at" by a coach, his daughter smiled and said, "She's not you. She's not my dad."

Dave has learned that children want unconditional love from their fathers. "Spend time with your children is what I will tell any father," he says. "My daughter's eyes light up and shine when she's with me." This light ultimately comes from God because Dave is fulfilling his covenant with his daughter.

Joanna has also learned many lessons. First, she says, she has learned to slow down: "We can get caught up in life and miss the joys of life."

As a single parent, she has also learned something else as well. Joanna has a lot going on in her life: two boys, sometimes two jobs, dating, church. These can all bring joy, but they can also bring problems and challenges, almost continuously.

Joanna says that the most important lesson she has learned is that "everything doesn't have to be okay for life to be okay." Life is full of adversity. You just have to accept that everything is not always going to be rosy and beautiful. Once you do accept that fact, once you slow down a bit, things start to get better. As Proverbs 21:5 says: "Careful planning puts you ahead in the long run; hurry and scurry puts you further behind" (MSG). And, of course, Joanna has learned to slow down by trusting God: "Come to Me, all you who labor and are heavy laden, and I will give you rest. Take My yoke upon you and learn from Me, for I am gentle and lowly in heart, and you will find rest for your souls. For My yoke is easy, and My burden is light" (Matthew 11: 28-30, NKJV). When she slows down, she has time to be "appreciative of the small things, like opening the window on a spring day and letting the fresh air come in."

Joanna says that if she had to give other single parents—especially mothers—some advice, she would say that "it's okay to be frustrated, and it's okay to ask for help." Of course, asking for help is just fine for single dads as well. But we live in a culture in which men are expected to be the captains of their destinies.

That's all well and good, but do not go down with the ship.

As a single mom of two boys, Joanna also believes that it is vital to get male mentors for her sons. In Joanna's case, her sons' father is not in their lives. This fact can be somewhat traumatic for the boys. At her oldest son's graduation party, he broke down crying because his father was not there. He still does not understand why. Joanna says that it is essential to be able to co-parent with the other parent. Unless there is abuse, you have created a child with the other person, and you two need to work together. You have entered into a covenant with this person, and you have to honor that covenant, just as God honors His covenant with you.

All in all, Joanna loves her two boys deeply, but she acknowledges that being a single parent is not easy. "You might want to sleep in on a Saturday, but you're not going to be able to because you have to be prepared to do things with and for your kids."

But remember, even though you might be on your own, you are not alone, especially if you follow the principles of the covenant family: grace, intentionality, empowerment, intimacy, and learning from life's lessons. Make these principles the guiding force of your family.

God is your copilot. He will not let you crash.

Bishop's Reflection

I hope that the experiences and insights of these two remarkable single parents, Dave and Joanna, will help you in your quest to honor your covenant with God and your children. I will be real with you: despite what culture tells us, being a single parent is not ideal for either you or your child. However, as a pastor, I know that people make mistakes and have to live with these mistakes. Now, your relationship choices might have been a mistake, but your child is not a mistake. Your child is a gift from God. Ideally, you should have a partner to share your burden with.

But you don't. That fact does not mean that all is lost and that your child is doomed to suffer. They are not doomed in any way, if:

- You make a covenant with that child, one in which God is your partner.
- You seek the proper support that you need.
- You create intimacy with your child.
- You actively parent your child.
- You do not surrender control of your child's upbringing to the internet.

These are a lot of ifs, but they are important ones. If you maintain your covenant with God and with your child, then your offspring can have a wonderful life, one full of joy, love, and success. No one ever said anything is easy, but with God, all things are possible.

Reflection Questions

1. What are your concerns about your child's television and social media habits?
2. What kind of plan can you develop to make social media work for you and your family?
3. If you are a single parent and you date, then what kind of screen do you have for potential partners?
4. If you are dating, then how do you make sure that your partner knows that they are important to you even though you have a pre-existing commitment with your child or children?
5. How do you maintain a covenant with your child's other biological parent?
6. How do you empower yourself, especially when you are facing challenges at home?
7. How do you take the time to appreciate the simple things in life?
8. Are you satisfied with the amount of time that you spend with your children? If you are not, then how could you arrange your schedule to spend more time with them?
9. What Bible verses inspire you as a single parent?
10. What are the unique challenges you face as a single parent, and how can you use your faith to overcome these challenges?

Chapter 4

Blended Families

'Til death do us part: Mom, Dad, and the kids.

One family forever.

Right?

Well, maybe.

Or, maybe not.

The traditional unbroken nuclear family is becoming more of a rarity in the United States. However, according to the 2016 U.S. Census, approximately sixty-nine percent of children under eighteen lived in a family with two parents. As I have mentioned previously, whether we like it or not, the divorce rates are high. Of course, many people who get divorced have kids as well. These kids come with the parents into another relationship or marriage. Multiple sources tell us that over two thousand blended families—with children from previous marriages or relationships—form every day in America. *Business Innovators Magazine* predicts and believes that the blended family will become the chief type of family unit in the United States (2015).

This fact represents a cultural change. I believe that the traditional nuclear family—one that stays intact—represents the best possible kind of family. It is the kind that I have and value. However, I recognize that the blended family is the reality for millions of people in the United States and perhaps especially in the African American community.

The blended family faces challenges that do not confront traditional families. For example, if you are a father in a traditional family, you know that your child's behavior is a combination of nurture and nature. You are at least partially responsible for both of those factors and have been since the child's birth. The same is not true for parents in a blended family. In addition, in the best possible circumstance, you planned for the arrival of your child; that is not the case in a blended family. Often, a child or children simply arrive as part of a package. These children can often be fully formed by the time you meet them. They do not have your genetics or your specific family culture, and you do not have theirs. On that same note, the children in a blended family often have a second birth parent to whom they are close. You may see yourself in competition with that birth parent—and you might be if you are not careful. That birth parent may have values and a parenting style completely different from your own.

In this chapter, I will share with you the experiences of Bill and Jennifer, who have done an excellent job of bringing together a blended family. They will share with you how they apply the principles of the covenant family in their lives. But first, I want to talk to you briefly about biblical principles. Both the Old and New Testaments were written long before the hookup culture, the massive rise in single parenting, and no-fault divorce. While there have always been blended families—and one might argue that Jesus lived in one since Joseph was not His birth father—the way we talk about them is new.

Does that mean that the Bible has nothing to say about this new kind of family? Absolutely not.

Both the Old and New Testaments are full of commands to take care of those needing care and nurturing. In Deuteronomy, we are told, "He defends the cause of the fatherless and the widow, and loves the foreigner residing among you, giving them food and clothing" (10:18, NIV). Clearly, the just person—man or woman—takes care of those who need him or her.

Let me tell you something: any child without both parents living with him or her needs you. Psalm 82:3 confirms this command to take care of children who might not be yours: "Defend the weak and the fatherless; uphold the cause of the poor and oppressed" (NIV). It is no secret that coming from a family that does not have two functional parents is a kind of poverty and oppression. We are called to behave as God behaved toward us. In 2 Corinthians 6:18, God says, "I will be a Father to you, and you will be my sons and daughters" (NIV). You are being called upon to be a mother or father to children who need you.

When you take on a new family, you make a covenant both with your partner and your partner's children. It is not a covenant to be taken lightly. You are forming a new family. You will need all the grace, intentionality, empowerment, intimacy, and wisdom that you can get.

All these qualities are found in Bill and Jennifer, a remarkable couple. Bill and Jennifer both have a military background. They are the proud parents of seven children: four boys and three girls. Bill has served as a deacon in our church. The couple together has helped other couples through the rough patches in their lives. They know that they are blessed by God and want to give back to others.

Chapter 4

Grace

Bill and Jennifer both believe that grace—the love they receive from God and the love they give to their children and each other—is the key to their success as a blended family. The Bible verse that steers their course as a family comes from Romans: “No, in all these things we are more than conquerors through him who loved us” (8:37, NIV). Bill and Jennifer understand that in an undertaking as complicated as bringing together two partners and seven children, all of whom have experienced disappointments as well as victories, grace is essential. In Ephesians, we are told, “For it is by grace you have been saved, through faith—and this is not from yourselves, it is the gift of God—not by works, so that no one can boast” (2:8-9, NIV). Bill and Jennifer are adamant: all things come from God.

Both Bill and Jennifer say that prayer comes at the center of their lives. Prayer for any family is important, but prayer for a blended family is crucial. As Romans says, “Be joyful in hope, patient in affliction, faithful in prayer” (12:12, NIV). In Psalm 4:1, we hear a lament, “Answer me when I call to you, my righteous God. Give me relief from my distress; have mercy on me and hear my prayer” (NIV). Trust me, as Bill and Jennifer know all too well, blended families will have distresses.

There are many issues that blended families face that traditional nuclear families often do not. For example, there is the issue of parent sharing. In a nuclear family, there may only be two or three kids. There may well be six or seven kids in a blended family, as is the case for Bill and Jennifer. Parents need grace to recognize that they will face greater demands on their time than parents in traditional families. You cannot be everywhere at once. Grace helps you to at least try to spend the proper amount of time with each child, making sure that they know that they are a welcomed and valuable member of the family.

Another issue for which grace is useful concerns identifying confusion and sibling rivalry that initially plagues nuclear families. In the case of Bill and Jennifer, putting so many kids together was a challenge. Bill and Jennifer overcame the challenge by emphasizing that they are *one* family. As we will see below, Bill and Jennifer were adamant that there would be no favorites in the family—everybody is a favorite. The ability to not discriminate among children takes grace and faith because there will be children you are drawn to more than others. It is not always the case that you favor your birth children. Remembering grace reminds you that everybody is God's favorite—and you have to play by God's rules. Value all your children—those of your new spouses as well as those you brought into the world. That job might not always be easy to complete, but your grace helps you get the mission accomplished.

Intentionality

Here's where the rubber hits the road in the blended family. Unlike the case in the traditional nuclear family in which children are related to each other by blood, the blended family must actually be intentional in being a family. That means spending time together. Bill and Jennifer recognize that they have a busy schedule, but they always spend as much family time together as possible.

As a father myself, I know that to be intentional about outcomes for my family, I have to know my family well.

What are they like? What are their strengths? What are their weaknesses? What are their goals?

I had an advantage that Bill and Jennifer did not have. I had been around both of my children since the moment they had been born. In developing your covenant with your family, the first step in intentionality is to get to know them. Spend time, as Bill and Jennifer do, having fun with your family. Play board games, watch family movies, talk about them afterward and listen to each member of your new family. You must figure out what makes each person tick.

After you know everybody—and hopefully you will have spent time with everybody long before you got married—you will need to figure out what your new family's mission is. What goal defines all of you? What is going to keep you together? What's your larger mission? How do you stay on task?

Your biggest mission is to help each other. You must help your kids and your spouse to fully develop themselves and prepare themselves for life both in this world and in the world to come. Then, as we have talked about for other kinds of families, what is the specific goal for your family? What is your mission? Are you a family of learners? Are you a family of do-gooders? Are you a legal family? Are you a literary family? You have a unique opportunity if your blended family includes teenagers from your partner. They can help you to determine your family's mission. They will need your guidance, but they can help as well.

In the Book of Matthew, we are told, "Therefore go and make disciples of all nations, baptizing them in the name of the father and of the Son and of the Holy Spirit" (28:19, NIV). In addition to your Christian mission, you have a family mission. You need to be as relentless about following this mission as you should be about being a Christian. Matthew's words also give us another clue about the mission of a parent in a blended family. Perhaps your new spouse has not been the best of Christians. They are a good person, but not a churched one. One of your family missions is to make all the members of your new family acquainted with the church and bring them into the church if they are not already there. You might say to yourself or me: "My new sons are already teenagers. Shouldn't I just let them be whatever they want to be?" My answer to that question is that if you follow that course of action, you are not intentional and faithful to your mission. These kids were brought to you for a mission. God gave you these children. He expects you to bring them up.

Before we move on to intimacy, I want to talk briefly about non-custodial parents. While Bill and Jennifer did not have any input from the non-custodial parents, and these non-custodial parents did not have any contact with the children after the couple's marriage, this state of affairs is not always the case. In either event, you are going to have some work to do. If the non-custodial parent is not involved in the child's life, then the child may be faced with haunting questions: "Doesn't my dad or mom love me? Doesn't he or she want me?" The only way forward here, from my perspective, is to say, "I don't know the answer to that question. But I do know an answer to another question: I love you. And I loved you so much that I chose to be with you. And I'm always going to be with you, just like your mom or dad is with you." Remember, the pain that this child may be going through because of perceived or actual abandonment may be profound. Be intentional here to express your love and commitment to this child, who may be desperately searching for the love of a parent of your gender.

Now, the opposite can happen. The non-custodial parent can be in the child's life on weekends, during the summers, or every other week. This experience may be hard for both you and the child. Be prepared for the following: one night, you ask your son to pick up his socks from the living room floor. He storms out. But before he does, he hits you with the following: "You're not my dad. I don't have to listen to you." This can be crushing. You have committed to being with this child. You have promised to love him as your own. As far as you are concerned, you are family every bit as much as you would be if you had helped conceive him. How do you deal with this? Well, there are no easy answers. However, you can say, "I might not be your biological parent, and I'm not trying to replace him, but I chose to be with you because I value you. And like it or not, when we're together, I'm the father of this family. This does not mean that you don't have a second father. You do. But we're a family unit. And I'm the head of it. The Bible tells us to honor our fathers and mothers. You are so blessed that you have two of them. And you have to honor both of us."

Remember, you have to be intentional about the expectations of your role and your new child's role as well. Be as clear as you can be. You will all benefit from your clarity.

Intimacy

Both Bill and Jennifer stress the need to develop intimacy. They recognized immediately that they were doing something rewarding but very difficult and rather unique: making a new family. With that comes busy schedules, requiring more effort to build intimacy. In addition to having family meetings, the couple also made sure that they had movie nights and Bible study.

Bible study is vital for any family. As the Book of 2 Timothy says,

---

> But as for you, continue in what you have learned and have firmly believed, knowing from whom you learned it and how from childhood you have been acquainted with the sacred writings, which can make you wise for salvation through faith in Christ Jesus. All Scripture is breathed out by God and profitable for teaching, for reproof, for correction, and training in righteousness, that the man of God may be complete, equipped for every good work. (3:14-17, ESV)

Bible study for a blended family is even more critical. Studying the Bible together is, first and foremost, doing something together. Second, it is making a statement to your new family that you want to be together and in the company of God. You are saying what and who is important to you. You are saying that God is the foundation of your new family—just as the Old Covenant with God was the basis of the people of Israel, and the New Covenant was the basis of Christ's relationship with His people. By doing family Bible study, you are sending a message: this is what we believe. This is who we are—who all of us are.

One of the reasons Bill and Jennifer's family is so well-blended is because of a policy that the two parents had from the beginning: "We are family. There are no steps here, just brothers and sisters, mom and dad." This policy is essential because it shows that there is unity and no differentiation between those who are born to one parent and those who are not. Everybody is equal. Everybody is family. Everybody is loved.

In terms of the couple's intimacy, Bill makes an exciting and funny comment: "We hang a hanger on the bedroom door when we want to be alone." While this trick certainly works and tells kids that it is couple's time for Mom and Dad, this is only the beginning of intimacy.

Bill and Jennifer often take "staycations." They stay home and spend time with each other. With seven kids to look after, they can both get exhausted. Both members of this couple have talked about how they form a good family management team. But sometimes, the members of the team need to recharge their batteries. Making sure that the intimacy between partners is solid is crucial.

In addition to the staycations they take, Bill and Jennifer say that keeping the lines of communication open between each other is necessary. It is important in a blended family couple to recognize that you both have done something pretty special: you have opened your home and heart not only to each other but to children who need another parent. Make sure you praise each other and communicate your love and admiration for your partner. Take some time to appreciate the love and work that each of you is performing.

The Bible is full of wisdom about the importance of a strong primary relationship. A relationship is the bedrock of a blended family. Ephesians 4:2-3 describes the ideal couple's relationship: "with all humility and gentleness, with patience, bearing with one another in love, eager to maintain the unity of the Spirit in the bond of peace" (ESV). Be patient with each other. Talk to each other. Express your admiration. In Ecclesiastes 4:9-11 (NIV), we are told that "two are better than one, because they have a good return for their labor; if either of them falls down, one can help the other up. But pity anyone who falls and has no one to help them up. Also, if two lie down together, they will keep warm. But how can one keep warm alone?" Beyond extolling the joy of cuddling, what these verses say is that a strong partnership helps both partners and helps them present a united front when dealing with what I am sure can seem like a small army of children. The warmth alluded to in these verses is metaphorical as well as literal. You will need the warmth to guard against the chill caused by children's illnesses, sibling rivalry, and the normal detritus of life.

Don't take your primary relationship for granted.

Empowerment

Blending a family takes time and energy as well as commitment. Besides love and dedication to your partner, you also need tools to help you all come together. Prayer is one of those tools. Involvement in one's church is another powerful tool that can help unify you. Bill and Jennifer employ these tools, but they also employ another: counseling.

Bill emphasizes that it is vital to blend slowly. You can't sit down and proclaim, "We're all family." Blending will not happen successfully unless you do the work. Bill and Jennifer did the hard work of bringing their new family together. One of the things they did use was family counseling. Bill and Jennifer say that family counseling was the "best foundation" they could have had. Not only did they all go as a family—each of the kids, who, of course, brought their issues into the new family, did individual counseling as well. The result, according to Jennifer, is that there are no lingering resentments or unresolved issues.

Bill and Jennifer say that one of the significant problems that newly blended families must face is the non-custodial parent's role in the new family. As I mentioned, in the case of Bill and Jennifer, the non-custodial parents had almost no participation in the lives of their children. Now, while on the one hand, this non-participation seems great because it makes the life of the new family a little less complicated, there is a dark side as well. Kids will bring unresolved issues with their non-custodial birth parents into their new family. As we see with Bill and Jennifer's family, counseling can help the kids work through these issues. It also helps with family communication issues. Professional counseling might not be for every family, but it certainly helped cement Bill and Jennifer's new family.

Learning from Life's Lessons

Bill and Jennifer also learned a great deal from their experience. They discovered that a traditional family is essential for the development of both girls and boys. Jennifer says, "I took a backseat in some ways and let Bill lead. He became the head of the household." But Bill is quick to point out that kids need both parents in a family. "We learned to complement each other," he says. There are just things that a parent of one gender can help with that a parent of another gender can try to but cannot be much help with. For example, Bill says that he knows about menstrual cycles, but he is not an expert because he does not experience them. Both mother and father contribute unique skills and abilities to the parenting relationship. Bill and Jennifer emphasize that they are a team, and they function like one, each bringing their abilities to the job of parenting.

In Proverbs, we are told the importance of wives and mothers in a household: "A wife of noble character who can find? She is worth far more than rubies. Her husband has full confidence in her and lacks nothing of value. She brings him good, not harm, all the days of her life" (31:10-12, NIV). Clearly, the Bible emphasizes the noble role of motherhood in the family. The Bible also emphasizes the role of fatherhood in the household: In Proverbs, we are told, "Hear, O sons, a father's instruction, and be attentive, that you may gain insight, for I give you good precepts; do not forsake my teaching. When I was a son with my father, tender, the only one in the sight of my mother, he taught me and said to me, 'Let your heart hold fast my words; keep my commandments and live. Get wisdom; get insight; do not forget, and do not turn away from the words of my mouth" (4:1-5, ESV). The Bible is clear. Both mother and father are necessary for a good, strong family.

Bill and Jennifer have said that while they have walked a tough road and have had to fight some little battles, they feel they have been very successful. They feel blessed to have abundance. They think other parents in similar situations can be successful as well. Bill and Jennifer give this advice to other blended families: "Blend as slowly as possible. Things don't happen overnight. It's kind of like pressure cooking a stew, slow and steady. It's going to take a lot of work and planning." But with planning and love, something tasty and nutritious will be served up.

Bishop's Reflection

I am impressed by Bill and Jennifer, a fantastic couple with an even stronger family. I want to share my perspective on blended families. While I am the head of a traditional family now, I grew up in an "old school" blended family. I say "old school" because I grew up when second marriages and blended anything was taboo in society and far-fetched in the church. My mother had three daughters. In the 1950s, that was not considered marrying potential. My father had a son. My mother and father gave their lives to Christ and then married. They received the social stigma often associated with blended families back then. Together, they then had seven more children. There was no room for eleven children in one house, so my three oldest sisters lived with my grandmother across the street. My father's son did not live with us either—he was a family secret. As the youngest, I was kept in the dark about the circumstances surrounding my parents' marriage and what took place before our family coming together.

To this day, our family discussions stop at a certain point. But there was one thing that was reinforced and drilled into us: we were one family, and there was no such thing as half-sisters. My three eldest sisters were treated as if my father—*our* father—was their father. We all had the same mother, and that was the glue that held us together even after all our parents died. My blended family was from another time, but we learned from the brokenness of our past.

Reflection Questions

1. How do you define a family?
2. If you are in a blended family, then how do you work to achieve unity?
3. What unique challenges has your blended family faced?
4. What role do non-custodial parents play in your blended family?
5. How can you find time to spend together as a family?
6. If you know a blended family, then how can you support them?
7. What prayers or Bible verses does your family use to solidify its covenant?
8. What kinds of issues does your blended family face?
9. How do you help all the children in your family to feel like brothers and sisters?
10. How do you take time to develop intimacy with your spouse?

Chapter 5

Special Needs Families

All families are special.

All children are special.

In fact, all people are special.

We are created by God in His image and given unique abilities.

That said, some families are blessed—and yes, I did say "blessed"—with members who are different in some unique way that requires extra care and loving.

Now, having said that, families with special needs children have two purposes. One, God gave the children to you because you have the ability to help them. God only gives us what we can handle. Or, perhaps, God only gives us what we can handle if we develop ourselves. Two, God gave the children to you to help change you in some way, to help you develop an ability or some special talent that would not exist without this child or these children in your life.

They are there for a reason, and so are you.

Often, we do not understand the reason why seemingly bad or difficult things happen. We see only crisis. But God sees something else: an opportunity to work out your salvation.

While his children were not special needs in a sense we will be talking about in this chapter, Job faced challenges that he did not understand. Job was an upright person. Job worshipped God, yet disturbing things happened to him: his children were killed, his wealth was taken away, and his health was devastated.

Job was in trouble, and he was confounded.

> Job spake and said, "Let the day perish wherein I was born, and the night in which it was said, 'There is a man child conceived.' Let that day be darkness; let not God regard it from above, neither let the light shine upon it. Let darkness and the shadow of death stain it; let a cloud dwell upon it; let the blackness of the day terrify it. As for that night, let darkness seize upon it; let it not be joined unto the days of the year, let it not come into the number of the months." (Job 3:2-6, KJV)

Because of the enormity of the situation, Job even questioned his existence: "Why didn't I die at birth, my first breath out of the womb my last?" (Job 3:11, MSG). Although his friends try to redirect Job from his bitterness, Job cannot be consoled and blames God for his difficulties. God responds directly to Job: "Why do you confuse the issue? Why do you talk without knowing what you're talking about? Pull yourself together, Job! Up on your feet! Stand tall! I have some questions for you, and I want some straight answers. Where were you when I created the earth? Tell me, since you know so much! Who decided on its size? Certainly, you'll know that!" (Job 38:2-5, MSG).

My point is this: Job does not understand why seemingly bad things happen—just as we do not know why people, including our children, are not the way we think they should be. But we did not create the universe. We did not order it. God did. We do not fully know His plan. But God knows what He is doing.

While our lives may be more challenging because of the presence of a special needs child in our family, there is a purpose for that child's existence and for our presence in that child's life. Through prayerful reflection, attention to personal discipline, and the support of like-minded family and friends, we can overcome anything. More importantly, we can use our difficulties as tools to make ourselves stronger.

God designs our plan and clarifies our assignment in His image and His divine goals for the world. Following as closely as we can to His wishes, we will see our way. Sometimes God's plan for us includes a special needs child.

Special needs children come in all shapes, sizes, talents, challenges, and abilities. The fact is that there are a lot of special needs children—millions. About eleven percent of the population of American children receive special needs educational services for a disability. A disability can be something relatively mild like dyslexia, or it can be something profound like Down Syndrome. The website *Verywell* argues that "'special needs' is an umbrella underneath which a staggering array of diagnoses can be placed. Children with special needs may have mild learning disabilities or profound cognitive impairment; food allergies or terminal illness; developmental delays that catch up quickly or remain entrenched; occasional panic attacks or serious psychiatric problems" (2018).

This chapter will introduce you to two parents who have two special needs children—one son with Asperger's syndrome and another with autism. I have also included a special section, "Supporting Parents of Special Needs Children." But first, I want to talk briefly about another kind of special needs child: the gifted child. About six to ten percent of children in this country are categorized as gifted. We are talking about an IQ range that starts at about 130.

On *Imperfect Parent*, an online magazine for parents, Kristina Ashlock writes, "When we think of a child with special needs, we tend to think of a child who is autistic, has ADHD, or suffers from dyslexia. Rarely does the gifted child come to mind" (2006). Ashlock, whose first-grader identified as having an IQ of 137, says that gifted children are often at risk. Because gifted children speak and think quickly, they are often misdiagnosed as having ADHD. Some of these children simply drop out of school because they become bored.

You might be scratching your head and saying, "Bishop, I thought you were going to speak about special needs children, not little geniuses." I *am* talking about special needs children, and gifted kids fill that bill as well.

"Special needs" encompasses a wide range of challenges, not all of which might seem like challenges. If you think about it from a perspective of faith, then problems can be gifts. Although we might not recognize this fact, gifts can often cause problems. For example, what if you have a daughter who has an IQ of 160? Genius levels begin at around 140. You might say, "Hey, Bishop, no problem. Let's sign her up for Harvard."

Your gifted daughter may very well be going to Harvard if she does not burn out first. Gifted children can get into a lot of trouble if they are not adequately challenged and mentored. What if she goes to Harvard at the age of fourteen? Are you ready for that?

We love to talk about gifted people like Bill Gates, Warren Buffet, and Salvador Dali. These are or were incredibly gifted people. But would you have wanted to have been their parent? I am not so sure. Salvador Dali, for example, tried to kill his sister when he was a child. How would you feel if your child were smarter than you are? We say that we want that, but the reality of the gifted child is another matter.

Also, consider the fact that your hypothetical daughter with an IQ of 160 might have a special ability like art, debate, dance, or science that requires a lot of time and a lot of money to develop. We could be talking about tens of thousands of dollars to develop that ability.

That does not even include college.

What about your other kids? Will they all get along? Your gifted child might resent her siblings because they cannot keep up with her. Maybe her brothers and sisters will be angry with her because they feel she gets more of your attention. This problem goes along with every kind of special needs child. You will recall the story of Cain and Abel. If you think about it, then that story is about an especially favored or gifted son, Abel, whose gifts were praised by God. A jealous brother killed Abel.

Having a gifted child might not seem like a special needs case, but it could also be much more of a challenge than you might think it will be. What about her emotional development? What if she is reading *War and Peace* at ten while her classmates are raving about the next Harry Potter movie?

What if she is challenging her teachers in front of the class? And, horror of horrors, what if she is right? What if, at seventeen, she is intellectually thirty-five but emotionally still a seventeen-year-old? What kind of guy is she going to be dating? Who is she going to want to hang out with?

My point is, special needs are that: special, out of the ordinary. People out of the ordinary require extraordinary care and concern. It does not matter if your special needs child requires you to feed him when he is fourteen or take him to science competitions. Both kinds of special needs children require your special concern.

Here's the great news: having somebody in your family with special needs will help you grow and blossom. What might seem a Job-like disaster is actually God giving you a fantastic opportunity.

Take it and run with it. You will never be the same.

As it says in Exodus 19:5-6 (NKJV): "'Now therefore, if you will indeed obey My voice and keep My covenant, then you shall be a special treasure to Me above all people, for all the earth is Mine; and you shall be to Me a kingdom of priests and a holy nation.' These are the words which you shall speak to the children of Israel."

Thus, whatever that child's special challenge in life is, the way you help your special needs child is by keeping your covenant with God and observing covenant family principles: grace, intentionality, empowerment, intimacy, and learning from life's lessons.

James and Liz are parents of two special needs children, one with autism and another with Asperger's. The younger son has autism and is almost nonverbal. The older son, who is about seventeen, has Asperger's. Let's take a look at how they apply the principles of the covenant family to their lives to become the fabulous family God called them to be.

Grace

As I often say when I preach, we can encounter challenges in faith. We are met by our own challenges on occasion, and on other occasions, we are confronted by the challenges presented to us by our children. Sometimes, these challenges are not deliberate, and they come in the form of work stress, illness or death in the family, or observations in our world that lead us to question who has our back in that vast universe out there.

When you have a special needs child, you will undoubtedly deal with faith challenges. Part of the challenge of having a special needs child is wondering, *Why me?* Like Job, you will doubt and gnash your teeth. Unlike Job, you have to remember that while you do not understand why your life has become complicated, you must believe God does have a plan. Sometimes we have to experience difficulties on the road to actualizing or realizing that plan. As Deuteronomy 31:6 says, "Be strong and courageous. Do not be afraid or terrified because of them, for the LORD your God goes with you; he will never leave you nor forsake you" (NIV).

If we apply daily prayer and worship in our families, and if we foster a sense of growth and learning within those families, then we will be able to handle any challenges that come our way—whether our own in times of great stress or grief, or those of others for any variety of reasons.

James and Liz use faith as their foundation in dealing with their special needs boys. Ironically, in keeping with the dictum that God never gives you more than you can handle, God provided James and Liz with a special foundation. James's father was a deacon, and Liz's dad was a preacher. In a real sense, James and Liz had a special spiritual inheritance. Ephesians 1:11-14 says,

---

> "In him we have obtained an inheritance, having been predestined according to the purpose of him who works all things according to the counsel of his will, so that we who were the first to hope in Christ might be to the praise of his glory. In him you also, when you heard the word of truth, the gospel of your salvation, and believed in him, were sealed with the promised Holy Spirit, who is the guarantee of our inheritance until we acquire possession of it, to the praise of his glory." (ESV)

There are many kinds of inheritances. James and Liz both have a precious one from their fathers. This spiritual inheritance would eventually help them keep their covenant with each other and their special needs children.

Liz says that Christ is the dynamic spiritual foundation of their family—the reason they are together. In a quest for strength, they both pray every day. James and Liz find special comfort and strength in Psalm 91. Verses 1 and 2 say: "Whoever dwells in the shelter of the Most High will rest in the shadow of the Almighty. I will say of the LORD, 'He is my refuge and my fortress, my God, in whom I trust'" (NIV).

As James and Liz know, God forms their foundation, one that will allow them to serve their children and grow as people themselves.

Intentionality

Being intentional in a special needs family is difficult. There is always something that will challenge the routine of a day. As James and Liz will tell you—you have to keep your eyes focused on the prize. This sounds easy, but it is hard. The prize, of course, is providing for your child while taking care of yourself. However, the prize often gets lost behind daily struggles—and there are many. Sometimes the struggles are so many they come hourly.

Liz says that you have to be "able to look beyond the now and see beyond it. At the moment, it's a challenge." Radical acceptance of the situation as it is, not as how you would like it to be, is crucial. Liz and James have had to face the hospitalization of their sons at certain points in the boys' lives. "Accept you are in this. Go to classes. Go to seminars. Be proactive. This is who you are. Accept it fully. God gave them to us," they say.

When the boys were small, Liz says, "We had to help them be able to communicate. We had to enter their world." Being intentional with a special needs child is about recognizing that child's differences. You may have to meet your child at least halfway.

You have to be proactive in learning to care and advocate for your child. You will face difficult situations but do not shy away from them. They are there to test you, to improve you. Like Job, maybe you do not understand why things are happening, but God is putting you in certain situations for your benefit. Embrace these situations. Liz says, "Stay the course. Be proactive." For example, one son had to go to counseling, and things were not going well at school. Physical restraints were being used on one son. "It's very difficult to be called by the school three or four times a week," Liz says. "I was in flight or fight mode." Liz and James were able to get through their crises by remaining intentional about their goals: the best outcomes for the boys. Because Liz and James stayed intentional, things improved. Their oldest son actually finished high school early and is in college now. The younger one is working on speech. Liz and James are working to make sure that the boys can be as independent as possible.

The prize is also working out your salvation. That's a big prize. Remember that God has put this special needs child in your life to help you as well as that child. Liz and James have developed as people through their experiences with their children. They have learned patience, resilience, and sacrifice. "Put family first. Depend on God," they say. "Raising the boys helped develop us. They taught us how to go above and beyond. God allowed us to develop a skill set. He made us compassionate and less judgmental and critical."

God can do this for you, too, in any area of life—if you let Him.

Empowerment

When you are helping somebody you love with special needs; you want to be there for them. You should be. But the reality is that special needs take special amounts of energy. You can become drained. In addition to having a strong church and spiritual life, you need to take care of yourself. That's true in any situation, but it is especially true in a special needs family.

I cannot stress enough the importance of getting plenty of exercise and staying in contact with family and friends. Keep your body and spirit in good shape to have internal resources that you can offer to your special needs children. These kids will need you, probably for a lot longer than most kids need their parents. Make sure you are healthy so that you can be there for them. Taking a couple of hours off from your caretaking responsibilities can help you feel refreshed and ready to deliver the best possible attention and care.

For Liz and James, getting outside and being absorbed in nature helps. They go on little "staycations" together, just the two of them, to get a little alone time. It is battery recharging time. It is also sometimes difficult for them to find babysitters, so they have learned to help each other. One will stay with the kids while the other works on a special or personal project.

One thing to keep in mind when you are dealing with special needs kids is that the whole process is draining for both of you. You have to learn how to decipher when your spouse needs help or time away. You can do little things for them, remembering that God chose both of you. Remember, the person next to you—your spouse—has been put there just as you have. Remember the uniqueness and worth of your partner through kind words and expressions of love—a vase of flowers here, a set of football tickets there. Remember, your partner is special. Empower him or her by recognizing God within this person.

In terms of frontline empowerment, there are several steps you can take. First, remember that you as parents are not alone. Join support groups with people who are on the same journey you are. These groups can be useful. Perhaps they will give you the comfort of knowing that others are experiencing what you are. God knows life can get very tunnel-like. You think you are alone. You're not.

Speaking of not being alone, make sure you connect with God. Pray daily. Liz and James do. You have to keep your covenant with God. If you keep this covenant, then you will discover an incredible resource: your fellow churchgoers. They are there to help. But they cannot help you if you are not at church.

Liz and James also learned about the importance of developing patience and perseverance. As it says in 2 Thessalonians 1:4-5, "We're so proud of you; you're so steady and determined in your faith despite all the hard times that have broadsided you. We tell everyone we meet in the churches all about you. All this trouble is a clear sign that God has decided to make you fit for the kingdom. You're suffering now, but justice is on the way" (MSG).

Parents of special needs kids definitely need patience. Success is measured in small steps. Sometimes the public schools did not seem to accommodate the boys' needs. Services were not always available, and sometimes, Liz says, it seemed as though the schools were trying to make the boys fit the school rather than the school fit the boys. Developing internal fortitude is crucial when helping special needs kids.

Intimacy

James and Liz spend a lot of time helping their boys, which demands a lot of their time. But when they are not helping the boys, James and Liz make sure to enjoy their time with the boys and with each other. At the beginning of the day, the family gathers, and James leads the family in prayer to set them up for the day. James and Liz take time to go on walks together. As a family, they often gather to watch *Family Feud*. All four of the family members enjoy the show and talk about what they are watching together. Occasionally, when they can, James and Liz sneak away to a hotel for a little together time.

While you may be in crisis mode sometimes when caring for a child, it is crucial that you love the child and each other. For couples, this experience of caring for a special needs child can place a lot of stress on your marriage, but it can also give you your sense of mission and purpose. Value both your special needs child and each other. Take time to grow your marriage, which is a source of your strength.

Learning from Life's Lessons

One of the biggest lessons for anybody to learn in life is who to trust. We can trust ourselves, our friends, and the professionals in our lives, but at some point, all of these people—including ourselves—will let us down in some ways. It's inevitable.

But there is one source that will never let us down: God. Learning to trust God is essential. This is a lesson James and Liz learned early on. As Liz says, "We learned to trust in God even when we can't see Him. We learned the power of prayer. We learned that it's good to sacrifice for family. And we also learned what it's like to make ourselves vulnerable."

Certainly, being vulnerable is not something we like to talk about in this culture. Americans want to see themselves as strong, but having a special needs child will convince you that you are not invincible. There will be circumstances that you cannot control—your child's needs, your child's behavior—

and you may need help from time to time. It's good to know what resources are available."

Early on, Liz and James learned that they are stronger together than they are apart. Difficult circumstances test us and make us stronger; they help teach us what is important. They learned how to be a fabulous family!

Supporting Parents of Special Needs Children

Thus far, you have gotten some good advice about what to do if you are a special needs parent, but this chapter is not just for special needs parents; it is for everyone. The chances are high that you will have somebody in your life with a special needs child. This somebody could be a friend, a sibling, or another relative.

Take this story from Liz and James. Their younger son, an adolescent at the time, demonstrated unexpected behavior that superseded their knowledge of the autism spectrum. After returning home from a powerful Easter service, their son's anxiety increased. He was triggered after inquiring about the location of a gaming system they had recently traded. Upon entering the house, he retreated to the basement, and James left to run an errand. Not long after, their son's anxiety escalated to the point that he became rageful and physically attacked Liz before she was able to barricade herself in the master bedroom. When he broke through the barricade and could not be calmed, Liz was forced to call 911. As Liz prayed and waited for help, their son began to terrorize the home with a hammer in a displaced emotional panic.

Wow. Intense.

While this situation is surely nothing to be ashamed of, it is most definitely frightening. This was part of his autism. He had had meltdowns before, but this topped them all. Thankfully, their son got the treatment he needed, learned to communicate his anxiety, and learned to implement better coping skills. Liz and James could have certainly used a friendly face in this situation. It just so happens that one of the police officers on the scene also had a son with autism. The police officer exhibited compassion when James and Liz needed it most.

Like most good people, when you see a need, you will want to respond. But the question is, how do you react in a way that does more good than harm? That is the challenge most people, including most churchgoers, face. Remember, offering this kind of support is part of our covenant with God. We have to be like the good Samaritan, offering help when needed.

Caring for special needs folks or supporting those who do often means caring for people we might not understand or even like. There will be times that you might not be thrilled with your special needs child or might even resent them.

But do you know what? God challenges us to take care of our neighbors, even those we might not like, every moment of the day.

In the Parable of the Good Samaritan, we are challenged to love those whom we might not always love and to recognize that our "neighbor" is anyone in our life who needs our help:

> On one occasion an expert in the law stood up to test Jesus. "Teacher," he asked, "What must I do to inherit eternal life?" "What is written in the Law?" he replied.

> "How do you read it?" He answered, "Love the Lord your God with all your heart and with all your soul and with all your strength and with all your mind;" and, "Love your neighbor as yourself." "You have answered correctly," Jesus replied. "Do this and you will live." (Luke 10:25-28, NIV)

If you think about it, Jesus is telling us to help those with special needs by being merciful and giving all the help we can.

Go and do likewise. It is not just the life of your child that's at stake. It is your soul, too.

Bishop's Reflection

James and Liz's story is inspiring. I learned firsthand what special needs and intimacy mean in my family of eleven. One of my five brothers is special needs. He has a low IQ and stutters. When we were growing up, society called him and others like him mentally retarded. On the playground, he was bullied, which was hurtful to all of us. We love our brother, and needless to say, we stood up to the bullies in the neighborhood to protect him. We still defend him. When my parents passed away, we assumed the responsibility of caring for him. My brother is entirely independent and can mostly care for himself. We have a covenant amongst us; someone will always take care of him. This covenant has created intentionality and intimacy. Loving Reginald has brought out the best in our family.

Before my father passed, on his deathbed, he said, "Geoff, take care of Reg." What a legacy of love and intimacy. Now Reginald stays with one of my sisters. He can take care of himself, and he does, but to make us feel good, he also lets us make sure life does not bully him.

Reflection Questions

1. How do you define "special needs?"
2. If you have a special needs child, how do you stay intentional?
3. How do you care for yourself while caring for a special needs child?
4. How do you create a sense of intimacy in your special needs family?
5. If you do not have a special needs family, then how would you go about helping a family that does?
6. How does faith play a role in your special needs family?
7. How do you think the presence of a special needs child in your family will help you to work out your salvation?
8. If you have a special needs child with a sibling or siblings, how do you make sure that the siblings feel cared for and loved?
9. If you have a gifted child, what is your plan for helping this child develop their gifts?
10. If you have a special needs child, what resources do you need to take care of this child and yourself?

Chapter 6

Parenting Adult Children

Raising kids is never easy.

You might assume that your job would be finished when the kids were out of the house. The truth is that parenting begins when your child is born, and it ends when you leave this world for the next.

Parenting is a lifelong journey.

As with any journey, parenting changes in nature when your children become adults themselves. You're no longer providing for their material needs—unless you choose to. You have moved into a different phase of your covenant with your children. The heavy lifting of parenthood is over. You have sown the seeds in raising your child. If you have done a good job, then your children will be healthy and happy.

In many ways, parenting can be like growing a crop. I am reminded of the Parable of the Sower:

> That same day Jesus went out of the house and sat by the lake. Such large crowds gathered around him that he got into a boat and sat in it while all the people stood on the shore. Then he told them many things in parables, saying: "A farmer went out to sow his seed. As he was scattering the seed, some fell along

> the path, and the birds came and ate it up. Some fell on rocky places, where it did not have much soil. It sprang up quickly, because the soil was shallow. But when the sun came up, the plants were scorched, and they withered because they had no root. Other seed fell among thorns, which grew up and choked the plants. Still other seed fell on good soil, where it produced a crop—a hundred, sixty or thirty times what was sown. Whoever has ears, let them hear." (Matthew 13:1-9, NIV)

Parenting is much like farming. You plant the seeds and try to protect the crops from all threats. If you are careful, then your seeds land in rich soil and yield solid and healthy children.

But even though you did a good job raising your children into adults, you still need to be there for them as they journey into adulthood, where they will run into all sorts of problems. Your kids may not require you to change their diapers, but they will undoubtedly need you for wisdom, advice, and sometimes help. While you may be ready to give help to your child, you must remember that this child is now an adult, a legal and moral equal. You have to respond to your adult child as an equal. Responding in this way may be difficult, but doing so may well be the difference between being a resource for your adult child and being considered condescending.

In this chapter, I will share some thoughts about maintaining your covenant family when your children become adults. I will also introduce you to two members of my church who are amazing parents of adult children: Dave and Marjorie.

Dave and Marjorie have had full and rewarding lives. Having been married for thirty-seven years, they have four adult children, including a set of triplets. Dave is retired from the Air Force. He and his family have lived in numerous places, including Las Vegas, Germany, Fort Walton Beach, Alaska, Honolulu, South Korea, Saudi Arabia, Paris, and Austria. Although Dave is out of the Air Force, he still does cybersecurity work. Marjorie is a homemaker and a church volunteer. Marjorie worked hard to create a great home for their kids.

Dave and Marjorie exemplify what it means to live the principles of a covenant family. Employing all the principles, they have good relationships with their adult children. I will share more about their story, but first, a little of mine.

Grace

We live in a millennial world, one in which young people—as many as fifteen percent of them—return to the nest that they flapped away from a few years before. One of the goals of any parent is to ensure that when their children fly the coop, they stay launched.

One way to ensure that adult children stay launched is to fill them with faith. The reality is that even if you fill your kids with faith, then you are going to need grace to keep sane when plans do not go your way and your adult child wants to come home again.

I remember when my son wanted to return to Atlanta to live. He had graduated from Morehouse College in Atlanta. My son felt his destiny was there. I thought otherwise. He reminded me he was a grown man and could make his own decisions. Even though he was grown and I wanted him to move on—as we were excited about being empty nesters—I did not feel that his destiny was in Atlanta, nor did I feel like he was ready to be on his own. In my view, college life in Atlanta was one thing, but making it on your own there was another. He insisted. Without a job and on an allowance from us, he forged ahead.

Over the next few months, our predictions became apparent to everyone in the family but him. To encourage him to give up the pipe dream, I took the vehicle we gave him in hopes he would give up. He did not. His life became more difficult. Our advice to him from one adult to another became a battle. Upon one trip to visit him, I was heartbroken to see him living in a rundown neighborhood and deplorable conditions. It became a test of wills, which I let him win even though he was losing. I gave him the grace to fail even though we were consumed with worry and prayer.

One fateful Sunday morning, he called and asked me to come to pick him up. After church, I drove straight there—eight hours—because I knew he was prone to change his mind. As predicted, when I arrived, he had changed his mind. At that point, my grace was gone. I was tired from preaching and driving. I made him come home. I forced him into the car, slammed the door, locked it, and sped off. He called the police on me while we raced down the road at eighty-five miles per hour or more. I told the police over the speakerphone in my car who I was and what I was doing. "You can come get me if you want to," I exclaimed, "but I am taking my son home." They did not come. I continued on our way. We argued most of the way until he fell asleep. Sixteen hours of straight driving. Two adults in total disagreement. Grace melted the divide. Now, grace had to prepare Glenda and me to lose our empty nest. Parenting never stops.

Dysfunction is normal.

I find it more alarming when the family does not know what is going on in their adult children's lives. I would much rather talk to an engaged family whose members know what is going on. Keeping the line of communication open through faith and unconditional love is critical.

Remember, parenting is an honor: "Behold, children are a heritage from the LORD, the fruit of the womb is a reward. Like arrows in the hand of a warrior, so are the children of one's youth. Happy is the man who has his quiver full of them; they shall not be ashamed, but shall speak with their enemies in the gate" (Psalm 127:3-5, NKJV). Of course, those arrows must be aimed carefully. That's the work of early parenting. Later parenting involves wisdom and unconditional love rooted in deep faith.

Intentionality

Now back to Dave and Marjorie's story.

One of the most important points that Dave and Marjorie stress is the observance of boundaries. They want to stay active in their children's lives, but they recognize that their adult children live in a very different world. Dave says, "We don't want to impose our morals on them." For instance, Dave and Marjorie got married at the ages of 22 and 21, respectively. "Our parents thought we were crazy," he says. But Dave and Marjorie understand that the roles have changed, and now they think their children are crazy for doing the things that are normal for their generation.

Dave and Marjorie want to guide their children, but they also recognize that they won't always agree with the children's decisions. Dave and Marjorie provide guidance, but they do not cross boundaries. Dave and Marjorie stay intentional and not reactive because they know that a wrong move can damage their relationship with their adult child.

As a pastor, I get many questions about balancing a family's first ministry—which is the home—with the real-life milestones that we all must face. It is easy to impose your morals and boundaries when your children are small because you are in control; you decide what they wear, what they should eat, and what you want them to believe about the world. From faith to how to treat people of different races and ethnicities, you instill what is right in your eyes into your children. From what college they should choose to what friends you know and like, you impose your expectations, hopes, and fears onto them.

But when children become adults, the parental role shifts from a benevolent dictator to a trusted advisor. You have to let go when your children become adults. You stay engaged, of course, but you must realize that your children will make their own decisions. When people become full adults, they exercise adult privileges, including making decisions. You have to respect that privilege. Accepting that they are going to make their own decisions also includes accepting that they are going to make decisions you might not like—decisions that have the potential to turn into mistakes.

Dave and Marjorie enjoy giving advice to their kids when asked. They have noticed that their sons and daughters tend to go to different parents for different kinds of advice. Dave gets the questions about finances and work, while Marjorie fields queries about matters of the heart. Dave remembers when his son Ben wanted to buy a new car. Dave's advice was that Ben should get a Subaru. A typical dad, Dave advocated for good mileage and reliable transportation. Ben wanted a

Charger because it would help him "get the babes."

What did Ben do?

After carefully weighing his father's sage advice, he bought the Charger.

Dave says that the purchase has negatively impacted Ben's life. He has had to replace the Charger since. But Dave recognizes that all you can do is give the advice you know how to give and then get out the way. As Dave says, "We give advice and want the best for you. All we want is your love."

As a pastor, I have experienced the same emotions toward young adults that Dave and Marjorie have. I give advice, but at the end of the day, people make their own choices.

Dave and Marjorie use social media to keep up-to-date with their adult children's lives. Both Dave and Marjorie agree on one crucial point: by all means, look at your children's Facebook posts. Keep up with the news. Like something, if you want to, but if you run into something on your adult child's social media page that you do not like, keep yourself in check and do not respond negatively.

If you do permit yourself to respond negatively, you might end up unfriended and on the outside, where you cannot do any good. You want to stay on the inside of your children's lives, even if doing so means you have to keep yourself in check in terms of responding. More than that, Dave says, you have to be careful not to overreact when your kids tell you something: "Just take in what they tell you. Roll with the punches."

Staying intentional is key to parenting at any stage, but intentionality is especially crucial with adult children.

Dave and Marjorie joke that they have always told their children that their goal for them is straightforward: "We want you to be taxpaying, law-abiding citizens with your own address. We want to come to *your* house and eat *your* food."

While humorous, what Dave and Marjorie are talking about is serious: they spent their lives working to create not only a great home but great kids. This endeavor took a lot of work and a lot of intentionality.

While Dave and Marjorie want their kids to be independent, they also understand that sometimes things happen. Together, they have a unique concept: the-get-out-of-hell-free card. Things can go wrong in life. Jobs can evaporate. Landlords can evict. Bad things can happen. So, Dave and Marjorie pioneered the get-out-of-hell-free card for just such an emergency. If one of their kids runs into trouble, they can go home for six months. Dave says, "If things go badly, you don't have to pay rent. You can save money. You can eat our food. The catch is, you need a plan. You have to go back out once you figure out what you want to do." Not only are Dave and Marjorie intentional in the way in which they interact with their kids, but the interactions themselves are also designed to help their children and encourage intentionality.

A brilliant strategy created by two great parents!

Empowerment

One thing that empowers Dave and Marjorie is that both came from strong, intact families. They both had strong parents. Dave and Marjorie modeled for their children what they learned from their families.

Dave and Marjorie say that one of the most important things they do as parents is attend church, take what they hear and read, and apply it to their lives. They both advocate for making sure that parents see scriptures as tools that you can give your kids. When your kids talk to you, you can listen and provide them with scriptural tools to apply to their problems.

Of course, problems happen. They always have, and they always will. The key is not to pretend that problems do not occur. Instead, it is to have a toolkit in place for when problems do occur.

Another tool to assist with fostering an adult relationship with your grown children is a strong relationship with your spouse. It is not easy to support an adult child, or any child for that matter, if you are not supported. Working on your relationship with your spouse may be one of the best things you can do to improve your relationship with your adult child.

Intimacy

Dave and Marjorie have made a firm commitment, a covenant, to remain in their children's lives and to share in those lives. Sometimes intimacy consists of sending a selfie as a check-in to see how things are going.

Sometimes, intimacy can be much deeper. One of their sons, Joe, had a child with his girlfriend. The relationship did not work out. Both Joe and the mother of his child, Becky, moved on. But Dave and Marjorie saw this as a chance to form a more intimate bond with their granddaughter and Becky.

The relationship between Joe and Becky offered Dave and Marjorie an incredible parental teaching moment. Dave says,

"We told both of them, no matter how you feel about each other now, you are connected forever through the child you made." Dave and Marjorie are proud that Becky and Joe share in parenting even though they are not together.

But Dave and Marjorie went a step far beyond what most parents of adult children would do, and they did so in a nonjudgmental way. Dave and Marjorie were incredibly gracious when they did not have to be. Proving that God never gives you more than you can handle, Dave was made an Elder in his church one Saturday. A desperate call for help came on the following Monday. Dave explains it like this: "God says you're elevated. And then He says, 'Put your money where your mouth is.'"

Dave and Marjorie did.

The call for help did not come from one of their triplets or their other child. It came from Becky. She called Dave and Marjorie in a state of panic. She was engaged to be married, but her fiancé had not been helping with rent. Becky and her daughter were about to be evicted. Dave and Marjorie did not hesitate. They extended their get-out-of-hell-free policy to the mother of their granddaughter. Becky and her daughter lived with Dave and Marjorie while she came up with a plan to go out on her own again.

Dave says, "Becky is in our lives now. She's a part of the family. She treats us like parents." The situation was made even more complicated because while Dave and Marjorie are black, Becky is white. Race did not matter to Dave and Marjorie. They heard a cry for help and responded. Dave says that even Becky's sister views Dave and Marjorie as parental figures.

Not only do Dave and Marjorie work to establish intimacy with their adult children, but they have also extended intimacy to a son's former partner. They did not worry about who was dating who. The mother of their grandchild was in trouble, and they stepped in. There is something wonderful about that.

Of course, Dave and Marjorie enjoy intimacy with their adult kids in non-emergency situations as well. On holidays, when all the kids come over, everyone begins to reminisce on their younger days. Dave and Marjorie will hear about things that happened in high school and wonder why they did not know about them when they occurred.

Some things will always remain a mystery!

Learning from Life's Lessons

One of the most important lessons that Dave and Marjorie learned is that you have to be patient with your adult children. They are still growing even though they are adults, and they still experience challenges in life, as we all do.

In addition to dealing with their son's lack of discernment in car selection, Dave and Marjorie have had to deal with some severe issues with their children.

For example, one of Dave and Marjorie's daughters had experienced—as many people do—a drinking problem. Instead of becoming angry, preaching, or threatening, Dave and Marjorie kept the line of communication open with their daughter and were fervent with their prayers.

Because they were patient and gave unconditional love, their daughter felt safe enough to talk with them about the problem. It had gotten bad enough that she had been drunk at a bar and had been slipped a roofie—a powerful sedative referred to as the date rape drug because it can coerce individuals into nonconsensual sexual intercourse. Fortunately, nothing unwanted happened, but the experience scared their daughter enough to quit drinking and start attending Alcoholics Anonymous meetings.

This unfortunate situation taught Dave and Marjorie a valuable lesson about listening to their children. If they are patient and simply listen, then they will be invited into their children's lives and allowed to be near their children's tender spots. If Dave and Marjorie are not patient or become judgmental, they will not be invited in, resulting in an inability to influence their children's lives positively. Nobody wants to be judged for their mistakes; everybody wants a listening ear, especially from their parents. Don't judge; listen.

Dave and Marjorie know how to act when it comes to their adult children. They know that there can and will be dysfunction in every family. Despite this fact, Dave and Marjorie see that you can still impart the appropriate wisdom to your children, just as Abraham experienced dysfunction and still accomplished his mission.

Perhaps the biggest lesson that parents of adult children learn is that your kids will always have some problems. No family—no person—is perfect. But if you have sown seeds with unconditional love and you keep the line of communication open, then you are in a position to positively impact the lives of your adult children.

When it comes down to it, that is what it is all about.

And, as a plus, you get to go to your kids' houses and eat *their* food!

Bishop's Reflection

I have learned my fair share of lessons with my adult children. I began learning about parenting adult children as an Air Force chaplain. I was sitting in my office in the chapel at the Spangdahlem Air Force Base, Germany, waiting for my next counseling appointment. It had been a long day, but I received energy from my call to counsel airmen and their families. Every day was rewarding to me. Little did I know that one of the most significant faith-and-family issues I would ever deal with would march into my office in a moment and completely drain me.

A young couple came in for premarital counseling. At that time, all couples stationed in Germany who wanted to get married had to receive some form of counseling. The couple sat down, looking like they had barely graduated from high school, and declared their love.

"Will you marry us?"

"Well," I said, "let's talk about why you came to see me as opposed to seeing your chaplain." I was a little suspicious about why they had driven such a distance—more than an hour—when they could have seen a chaplain where they were. Was it because they were so young?

As usual, I began to break the ice with small talk. As we chatted, I noticed him holding her hand, and with every probing question I asked, he gripped her hand more tightly.

Probe.

Squeeze.

Probe.

Squeeze.

So even though I was afraid that he might cut off her circulation, I began to probe even more deeply.

"Why do you want to marry? Do your parents approve? Do you know that it was God who instituted marriage?"

Bingo! Bam!

My probing hit the problem.

It was not their age.

It was his faith. He identified as both agnostic and Wiccan. Obviously, I saw a problem here. And so did he, actually.

By this time, he was squeezing her hand so tightly that she was squirming. I could see that her hand was as white as a piece of paper with his fingerprints in red on the backside.

What was going on?

He had no faith, and she did. Her family, friends, and minister were totally against their marriage, but she loved him. As a chaplain in the U.S. Air Force, my dilemma was that I could not force my faith on anyone.

In the pluralistic world of the military, all faiths are valid and must be respected. I wondered what to do. Everything in me wanted to shout "NO!" as every other person had. Since I served in the Air Force, I should give you an aviation metaphor for my thoughts. My day, which had taken off so perfectly, was now spiraling downward and was about to crash and burn.

Instead of jumping up and down and yelling at these young people—which would not have done much good—I used the language of the young man's confused faith to help them see that there were some real problems in terms of compatibility. He never loosened his grip on her hand, and in a metaphorical sense, I'm not sure he ever did.

The young couple left as they had come: seeking.

My point is that I had advised these young adults to consider the consequences of a marriage without a shared faith. They had to make their own decision. Even though I respected their adulthood, I remained intentional with them in my final analysis because I did not want them to make a mistake.

Generally, with adult children, less is more. Under-reaction is usually better than over-reaction, which can shut down communication in a heartbeat.

Chapter 6

Reflection Questions

1. If you still have children at home, then how do you see your role in their lives changing after they leave the nest?
2. If you have adult children, then how do you advise them?
3. What dysfunction have you noticed in your adult children's lives, and what kind of advice do you give? Has that advice worked? If it has not, then what would you do differently?
4. How do you maintain intimacy with your adult children?
5. What Bible passages can you turn to for empowerment in your relationship with your adult child?
6. How do you roll with the punches when your adult children tell you things that you might not want to hear?
7. How would you respond if your adult child told you about a major problem like alcoholism, drug addiction, or financial distress? Is it a helpful response? If not, then how could you change your response?
8. How do you use your faith in God in your interactions with your adult children?
9. How do you practice patience in your relationship with your adult children?
10. How do you employ unconditional love with your adult children?

Chapter 7

Caring for Aging Parents

"Honor your father and mother." We have all heard these words from the Ten Commandments. But what do those words mean?

Perhaps you think they mean that when you are young, you need to listen to what your mom and dad tell you. Well, you are right about that. You might also think that when you leave home for college or a job, you are on your own, and so are Mom and Dad.

So long, folks.

Your duties are done.

Right?

Wrong. The commandment to honor your mother and father is a lifelong commitment. Your parents made a lifelong commitment to love you unconditionally. Your duty to them is also lifelong.

And that life might be very long.

Today, we are living longer than we ever have.

Orange may be the new black, but eighty-five is the new sixty-five.

That is good news since God is happy when we use technology and medicine to learn to live longer and enjoy His Creation. Nothing wrong there. However, the odds are that the longer we live, the greater the likelihood that we will become ill or need help.

The statistics support my argument. More than 65 million people—about a third of the population—provide care for an ill or aged family member or friend during any given year. These folks spend twenty hours per week as caretakers (National Alliance for Caregiving in collaboration with AARP, 2009).

That's like having a second job.

So, given these realities, there is a high likelihood that you will be called upon to care for an aging parent at some point in your life. You may see this duty as a burden. You shouldn't. You are receiving an opportunity to help someone who brought you into the world, cared for you, and gave you unconditional love.

Do you not think it was unconditional love? They changed your diapers. As a father, I can tell you that is about as unconditional as it gets.

By giving back, you are fulfilling a part of your covenant with your parents.

Some of you might completely agree with me and say, "Bishop, my parents were great. They were always there for me when I needed them. It's my duty to help out. Bring it on."

That is wonderful, but I will caution you that this duty may take a lot out of you. Remember what you were like when you were a child? You needed a lot of attention, and your aging parent might as well.

In this chapter, you are going to hear from Pam, a strong woman in my church who responded to the call from God to help her mother when she needed assistance. Pam is still helping her mother, fulfilling the covenant she has with her mom. We will also have a special section, "Helping the Unlikable," which focuses on helping aging parents who have not always been the best parents.

Pam's mother, Denise, has Alzheimer's disease. One of the strange things about people living longer is that the probability of Alzheimer's increases as we age. The Alzheimer's Research Association (ARA) notes that the U.S. population is rapidly aging. The number of people who are age sixty-five and older will more than double between 2010 and 2050 to 88.5 million. That's twenty percent of the U.S. population (ARA, 2014). According to the U.S. Census Bureau, the number of those eighty-five and older will rise to 19 million (2014). Right now, about 5.1 million people over the age of sixty-five have Alzheimer's Disease, and more than half a million people under the age of sixty-five have early-onset Alzheimer's Disease (ARA, 2014). Alzheimer's can strike anybody, even knights in shining armor. I can tell you countless stories of unstoppable people who were diagnosed with Alzheimer's.

So what is Alzheimer's? The disease has been around since time began. If you have ever heard the term "second childhood" in Shakespeare, then you have listened to a phrase that can be equated to Alzheimer's. The disease impairs cognitive functioning, destroys short-term memory, and creates a state of dementia, of not knowing what is going on or where one is. Alzheimer's can come on slowly—so slowly that friends and even spouses do not quite understand what is happening. A similar condition, vascular dementia caused by a stroke, can occur instantly.

In any event, a significant possibility exists that at some point in your life, you may be caring for a parent who is experiencing some form of dementia.

How do you cope with a parent with dementia or even another less debilitating illness or circumstance?

Well, you can apply the principles of the covenant family to your relationship with your parent in need: grace, intentionality, empowerment, intimacy, and learning from life's lessons. These are the principles you can use to make helping an adult parent not just a task but a mission—and it will help you as well.

In 2003, Pam began to notice something strange was happening with her mom. One day, Denise took off and was found by a member of Pam's church just wandering down the street. The church member took Denise to Pam's aunt's house. Then, on a trip to Virginia with Pam and her husband (Dave), Denise stayed in the cabin next to Pam and Dave's. Denise wandered off in the middle of the night and ended up at Pam's cousin's house. In addition, Pam, who had power of attorney for her mom, discovered that Denise was going to the bank and taking out hundreds of dollars at a time for no particular reason.

After these incidents, Denise was diagnosed with Alzheimer's. This diagnosis was particularly heartbreaking for Pam since she was an only child. Only children tend to have a close relationship with their parents. Denise was Pam's only surviving parent. Most upsetting for Pam was that in her working life, Denise had been a teacher—someone who had it all together, was in charge, and was brilliant. It was hard for Pam to see a woman who had supervised hundreds of children lose a large part of who she was.

Lots of people go through an experience like this one. But what is different about Pam's experience is the way she responded. She did not see the onset of Denise's Alzheimer's only as a tragedy. Pam saw it as an opportunity to give back and fulfill her part of the covenant she had with her mother.

Pam did not get angry at God for the situation. She applied the principles of the covenant family to her relationship with her mom.

Grace

Let's take a look at what the Bible says about your responsibility to your parents.

In the Book of Deuteronomy, we are told that honoring our parents is key to our spiritual journey: "Honor your father and your mother, as the LORD your God commanded you, that your days may be long, and that it may go well with you in the land that the LORD your God is giving you" (Deuteronomy 5:16, ESV). We can interpret the "land that God is giving you" in two ways. First, we can see it as the land given by God to Israel as part of the Old Covenant. Second, we can see this land as the promised land at the end of our lives. How we treat our parents is part of us getting to heaven. The Book of Proverbs is much more specific about what it means to honor our parents: "Listen to your father who gave you life, and do not despise your mother when she is old" (Proverbs 23:22, ESV). We have a biblically based responsibility to our parents. This responsibility can be weighty. But God always gives us the tools that we need to carry out any task.

In much the same way that we can bring stray family members back to God, we can also work through life's greatest challenges—illness, death, infidelity, and other sorts of loss. If the void left by these challenges and losses is filled with God, the Holy Spirit, and an individual's sense of their role as a Christian, restoration is much easier.

I am not saying that it is easy to overcome something like the death or illness of a loved one, but I am saying that we can overcome these monumental challenges when we ensure Christ is at the center of our lives. We must trust that what He is instructing us to do will be enough to get us through and provide us with peace and healing.

Pam says that her faith was vital in coping with the challenge that God had given her. God's Word provided her with a great deal of support. God was on her side. She recognized that, as Philippians says, "I can do all things through Christ who strengthens me" (4:13, NKJV). Some moments certainly necessitated a great deal of strength, such as having to deal with the bank when her mother was making large withdrawals and not remembering those withdrawals. Pam knew that no matter what happened, she had a friend in Jesus. Pam knew that when we are faithful to God, we receive what we need.

Beyond all of this, Pam recognized an essential element of her ongoing experience with her mom. God will do things that help us, but there is also something else going on. While we cannot fully understand God or what He has in mind, everything works for His glory as well as for our good.

That is a difficult concept to wrap your head around, but Pam got it. The problem is detailed in the story of Job. Job had many issues: the death of his children, his health, and the wiping out of his fortune. Job, who had been faithful to God, questioned why these seemingly bad things were happening to him. God responded to Job by telling him that

He was not accountable to Job. We might not understand why something is happening, but God does, and He does not always tell us why. He told Job that He did not have to tell him why, and so many times, God says the same thing to us. There is a reason for the occurrence. We have to radically accept the reality of an event and then choose our response to the occurrence carefully.

Pam's response to the storms of life and the ocean of dementia in which her mother was floating was simple: she accepted, and she prayed. Pam's faith prepared her to take on some large tasks, ones that might have been unbearable without the help of God.

Intentionality

Denise's Alzheimer's presented some enormous challenges. Pam's faith helped her to be intentional.

The parent-child roles had reversed. Pam, who was still working, now had to step in and become, in a real sense, the mother of the relationship. Pam says, "I was an only child. My mom had sisters, and they were great, but this was my responsibility. I had to take care of my mom."

One of the things Pam had to do was seek guardianship of Denise so that she would be able to make decisions about her mother's care. Guardianship also allows the guardian to responsibly use the ward's finances to care for the person. Guardianship is a big responsibility. You become responsible for the well-being of the person you are caring for. It is a complete legal reversal of the concepts of adult and child. It is such a profound responsibility that you have to report to a court every year about the person's well-being and finances.

Courts take guardianships seriously. It is not a responsibility to be taken lightly.

Pam did not hesitate for a second in getting guardianship. She was intentional and showed that she would do what it took to take care of her mother. It was about giving back.

Fortunately for Pam, her husband Dave walked alongside her on this journey. Dave had always said that if one of their parents became ill, then their house would be the parent's house. Thus, Denise moved in with Dave and Pam. Dave even made the noble sacrifice of his "mancave" so that Denise would have her own space.

Let's be honest. This experience was a heavy burden to bear. It was emotionally heartbreaking for Pam to see her mother reduced. She could not believe it happened to her mom, an educator and student of the Word. But she had to accept it.

Once she achieved that acceptance, Pam focused like a laser on taking care of her mom. "I had to honor my mother; it was my responsibility. And I was thankful to my mother," she says.

This thankfulness was the core of being intentional for Pam.

Now, one thing to keep in mind in being intentional about caring for an aging or ill parent is that when you do engage in care, it is likely that you will be engaging for a long time. This is not a romantic television-style rescue that is over quickly. It is more like wandering through the desert with someone. Parents can be ill or suffering from Alzheimer's for years or even decades. Part of being intentional is recognizing the scope of what you will be undertaking and ensuring you have the proper support from God, family, friends, the church, the wider community, and, where appropriate, the correct government agencies.

In the Gospel of Luke, Jesus asks, "Suppose one of you wants to build a tower. Won't you first sit down and estimate the cost to see if you have enough money to complete it?" (Luke 14:28, NIV). Christ is not telling you not to care for your parents if you do not have money. But what Christ is suggesting is to plan carefully when you start taking care of your parents. You need to have staying power, so prepare yourself for the long haul. Preparation is part of intentionality.

Empowerment

For Pam, empowerment took many forms. Of course, she was empowered by her faith in God and by the wisdom and compassion of her husband. Her friends and fellow church members also empowered her. One of her girlfriends had been through a similar experience with her mother and provided the right kind of support—grounded in shared experience—that Pam needed to make the right decisions for her mother and herself. Pam is the choir director at her church. She was able to bring her mother along to both the church and choir rehearsals.

Making sure that you have the right kind of support is critical for getting through circumstances such as the ones Pam found herself in. For example, Pam used adult daycare for her mother for several years. This service helped Pam and Dave to continue to live their lives and perform their work roles. Always make sure that you know what services, both in your networks and in the broader community, are available to you.

Chapter 7

Intimacy

You might suspect that Pam dealt with a whole host of issues during her time caring for her mother, and you would be right. You might not suspect that Pam also found the opportunity for intimacy and connection with her mom. An only child, Pam had had a good childhood and was close to her mother before the onset of dementia. Her mom had always given her advice that was grounded in biblical wisdom. She even used a biblical concordance to look up the meaning of a particular biblical passage. If Pam had had a rough day, Denise would counsel her to pray. The two women had enjoyed a strong, biblically informed relationship.

But even after the onset of dementia, Pam could still talk to Denise. Sometimes, the dementia produced funny results. Once, when Denise saw Pam and Dave hugging and kissing, Denise said, "Pam, you shouldn't be doing that with your father." Dave and Pam burst out laughing. In the nursing home, Denise would often remember things from the past. She retained some of her skills as well. For example, a former teacher would correct people's grammar. Once a teacher, always a teacher.

While the Denise of Pam's childhood was, in some ways, gone, there was still an opportunity for Pam to connect with her mother and share laughs and even a few tears. If caring for a parent is a biblically mandated responsibility, that responsibility also gives the caretaker some gifts, including a chance to have a different kind of relationship with one's parent, one that is based on giving back.

Learning from Life's Lessons

Pam learned a great deal during her time caring for her mother. One thing she knew was that she needed to embrace change. When her mother first started having memory problems, Pam kept thinking, "This will get better." She was hopeful. Then, she eventually began to realize that her mother's condition wasn't going to improve. Someone had once said to her, "You still have your mother." Pam says that while in a physical sense that was true, in a much larger sense, the mother she knew was gone, replaced by somebody else who looks like her mother and occasionally acts like the mother she knew. Often Pam's mom is somewhere else.

It's not that Pam had to give up hope. It's that what she needed to hope for had to change. Denise's Alzheimer's was not something Pam could control. Indeed, even with the level of medicine in the United States, which is very advanced, doctors cannot control or reverse the dementia Denise suffers. Thus, Pam couldn't continue to hope for Denise's recovery from the dementia. Did that fact mean that Pam had to stop hoping?

Of course not.

Her hope had to change and mature, though. It would have been too easy for Pam to become like Job: "Where then is my hope—who can see any hope for me?" (Job 17:15, NIV). Pam learned to hope for perseverance and dedication, and faith that God was leading both her and Denise through the desert into the promised land. Romans explains this kind of hope well:

> "We boast in the hope of the glory of God. Not only so, but we also glory in our sufferings, because we know that suffering produces perseverance; perseverance, character; and character, hope. And hope does not put us to shame, because God's love has been poured out into our hearts through the Holy Spirit, who has been given to us. You see, at just the right time, when we were still powerless, Christ died for the ungodly." (Romans 5:2-6, NIV)

Pam could and does hope for the wisdom, courage, and love to help Denise in this time of her life.

Pam has learned through taking care of Denise that she has to be careful of who she takes advice from when dealing with a difficult or specific situation. Many people give well-meaning advice, but if the person giving the advice hasn't been in the particular situation you're in, the direction may end up missing the mark and perhaps even causing more harm than good. Be careful who you listen to for advice.

Pam has also gained wisdom from her experience caring for her mom. You have to be aware of your limitations and the scope of your problem. For example, Pam and Dave were happy to have Denise live with them for about six years. But after that time, Pam and Dave realized that even with the help of friends and services such as adult daycare, Pam's level of dementia was simply too high for them to deal with. Thus, Pam and Dave made the tough decision to place Denise in a nursing home.

Helping the Unlikable

Now, some of you might be thinking, "Bishop, my parents were terrible. They didn't care for me. They weren't there for me. They abused me. I haven't seen my father since I was twelve, and now he wants my help? Why should I give my support to anybody who abused me?

That's a great question. On the surface, your response is reasonable.

But if we dig down a little bit, you're being allowed by God to try to heal the relationship between your parent and yourself. That's a gift—one you should not turn down. That's where grace comes in.

I don't pretend for a second that this opportunity might not be challenging for you, but I do think that it's worth pursuing. "Honor your father and mother" is not a conditional command. God is very direct. There are no exceptions, even if your parents didn't fulfill their responsibility. If you don't help, who will?

Let's be honest, though.

How do you honor that commitment when you've been abused mentally, physically, emotionally, and even financially?

With the onset of drug addiction, crack in the inner city, and meth in the suburbs/rural America, abusive parenting has increased exponentially. *Psychology Today* reports that child abuse rates have increased. There seems to be a correlation between opioid use and child abuse (*Psychology Today*, 2016).

Seventy-nine percent of child abuse cases involve abuse by the child's parents. And, while this fact may seem astounding, fifty-four percent of the parental abusers are mothers (*Psychology Today*, 2016). Believe it or not, to support their addiction, some parents even use their child's social security number to open accounts and receive benefits.

How does a child honor parents who dishonored their credit history and might have engaged in an assortment of other abusive behaviors?

Intentionally forgive. Like *love*, *forgiveness* is a verb, not a feeling. According to Matthew, you should forgive as God has forgiven you. You have to intentionally forgive them, and you have to walk in grace toward them. There is no more consolation. Jesus gave us sufficient grace for a new relationship both with God and with others in our lives.

You will be empowered by the Holy Spirit, and by the Holy Spirit you will exceed your expectations when it comes to honoring your abusive parents. You will increase intimacy by opening up the lines of communication with your parents. If you need to, you can even write a letter to your parents, expressing your feelings. Whether you send the letter or not is up to you, but writing such a letter can help you to forgive and to clear your head so you can be in a position to honor your commitment and help your parent.

I understand that the forgiveness you need to engage in will not be easy, but forgiveness never is. It's a process—one you're being invited to start—and you can bring some light to what has been a pool of darkness. Remember, the call for help is also about you. This experience, while certainly difficult, can provide you with benefits, too. In the Parable of the Good Samaritan, Jesus tells us that we have to love our neighbor as ourselves. Now, the catch here is that Christ never explicitly says who our neighbor is. The reason He doesn't is that everybody is our neighbor. The call to love is unconditional. Jesus washed everybody's feet. Even when Peter didn't want his feet washed, Jesus convinced him otherwise. You have to face God eventually. Did you do everything He called upon you to do?

Sometimes the best gifts in life come wrapped as problems, in which bitterness becomes transformed into blessings. I invite you to unwrap what you've received. No matter how much or how little. You might be surprised at what is inside.

And you know what?

Your act of caring for a parent might help heal your relationship with him or her.

Bishop's Reflection

I'm amazed by Pam. She encountered a situation that would be difficult for anyone and tragic for most people, and she did very well. She did so well because she took care of herself and applied the principles of the covenant family.

While deciding on placing a person in a nursing home may seem selfish, it truly isn't. Sometimes an aging parent or other family member needs a level of care that the family can't provide. One thing to keep in mind is that caregivers tend to get sick themselves from overwork and lack of self-care. It's like they say on airplanes: put your oxygen mask on first before you try to help someone with theirs. It's certainly not an easy decision to make, placing a loved parent in a nursing home. But sometimes, it's the necessary one. Be open to change.

Caring for an aging parent isn't easy, especially when their health is failing. It is draining emotionally, financially, and spiritually. In the last months of my father's life, it was difficult watching him decline from the strong man I knew and admired to a frail man dying from prostate cancer. I flew home once a month and sat at his bedside from Thursday to Saturday. One time, the last time, while he could still talk, he asked me why they were not treating him. Apparently, my siblings had not told him he was terminal. I did. I walked out of the hospital room after I told him. I broke down and cried. He cared for me, and now I had cared for him—completely drained.

Whenever you care for somebody else, make sure you care for yourself as well. A large part of caring for yourself is ensuring that you're spiritually healthy. Pray daily. Keep in close contact with friends and loved ones. Nurture yourself so that you can nurture others.

Reflection Questions

1. How can caring for an aging or ill parent be a gift for you?
2. What do you think your responsibility to your parents is?
3. If you are caring for your parents, what scriptures give you strength?
4. Why are prayer and self-care important when caring for a parent?
5. How could caring for a parent be a way to improve your relationship with that parent?
6. How can you be intentional in caring for your parents?
7. If you've cared for or are currently caring for a parent, what moments of intimacy have you had with your parent?
8. If you've cared for or are currently caring for a parent, what life lessons have you learned?
9. How do you overcome a bad relationship or no relationship at all with your parents who need care?
10. If you have cared for a parent, how has the experience shaped your view of the meaning of aging?

Chapter 8

Financial Issues in the Fabulous Family

In Matthew 19:21-24, Jesus told a young man,

> "If you want to be perfect, go, sell your possessions and give to the poor, and you will have treasure in heaven. Then come, follow me." When the young man heard this, he went away sad, because he had great wealth. Then Jesus said to his disciples, "Truly I tell you, it is hard for someone who is rich to enter the kingdom of heaven. Again I tell you, it is easier for a camel to go through the eye of a needle than for someone who is rich to enter the kingdom of God." (NIV)

You might read this passage from Matthew and scratch your head. You may say to yourself, "Well, Bishop, I've got this one covered. I don't have two nickels to put together. And what does money have to do with my family anyway?"

Family and finances go together hand in hand. Money. We need it. We want it. We do not have enough of it.

The financial picture of most people in the United States is pretty bleak. While, as a whole, the United States is one of the wealthiest nations in the world, individually, most of us are not rich. True, Bill Gates, Warren Buffett, and the Walton clan exist. Each of these outliers is worth billions of dollars.

Most of us do not have a lot of money. The median household income in the United States in 2016 was about $59,000, according to the U.S. Census Bureau in 2017. Per capita income—what each person receives—is lower. Statistics in 2008, the last figures released, indicate that the overall median per capita income is about $32,000. That number is lower for African Americans, who earn about $27,000. Perhaps the most frightening statistic of all was released by CNBC in September of 2017, which reports sixty-nine percent of families could not come up with $1,000 in cash immediately for a relatively small financial emergency. This fact means that most Americans stand one missed paycheck, or broken transmission, away from severe financial trouble.

Despite the stock market's recovery since the meltdown of 2007-2008, things probably will not get a lot better for most Americans. In 2013, the French economist Thomas Pikkety wrote a seminal work entitled *Capital in the Twenty-First Century*. In this book, Pikkety preached that the economic state of affairs in the United States is reverting to what it was in the 1890s, before the GI Bill and The New Deal of the twentieth century. About ninety percent of the population will just get by, and ten percent will enjoy inheritances and the security of such intergenerational wealth transfers.

Welcome to the new Gilded Age.

Financial problems take their toll on Americans. Finances are the number one reason for divorce in the United States. Not infidelity, not in-laws, not problem children. But money.

If the economy itself is problematic, then the cultural difficulties increase exponentially. We live in an age of late capitalism—a period driven by consumer spending and consumer overspending. Our television, billboards, and social media tell us that to be happy, we must spend more and push ourselves into debt to buy the latest smartphone, car, computer, sneakers—and the list goes on.

It is almost as if the culture invites us to buy our way to heaven.

We can't.

Money is a tool—a beneficial one. It can put a roof over your head. It can put food on the table. It can put your kids through college.

But it cannot get you into heaven. Neither can your smartphone.

It does not matter if you know your family's mission or have the money to enable and empower the mission's goal. When you do not know your purpose, you spend your life away with the bit of money you have. Money has a purpose, and it will attach itself to a person with purpose.

I have yet to meet anyone who purposefully wanted to be broke and destitute. I have never met a person that was happy being in debt and struggling to pay their bills. I have yet to meet someone who was delighted that they could not go out to dinner, take a vacation, purchase the clothes they wanted, or give as much as they wanted to their church or a favorite charity. We all want to live comfortably, but how do you get to that level of living? You have to live a life of purpose when it comes down to your family finances.

It starts with embracing the fact that our families live in the providence of God. What does that mean? Providence means God is sovereign and is deeply committed to those who live under His rule. Think of a country, state, or city with jurisdictional limits. Within that country, state, or city, its citizens can expect certain things when they pay taxes and obey the laws. They can expect protection, roads, access to electricity, power, and water, and parks for recreation. They can expect those with governing authority to afford citizens the right to "Life, Liberty and the pursuit of Happiness." God is the ruler of His Providence. He gave us dominion in His kingdom through Adam and Eve—the first family—and then through Jesus Christ. Our families live in God's Providence. When we comply with the rules of His Providence, we should expect His providential care.

There is dissatisfaction with the things you buy without purpose and a budget. When we fail to love God with our whole heart, mind, and body, it shows in the things we buy. The purchases are frivolous without meaning. They are tempered. Live within your means and set your family on the path from living in "not enough" to "just enough" to "more than enough."

In this chapter, we will talk about money and spirituality. We will talk about how you can use the principles of the covenant family to learn to use money and not be used by it. Grace, intentionality, intimacy, empowerment, and learning from life's lessons will help you and your family deal with money issues so that you can be a genuinely fabulous family.

Grace

The first thing to remember about our time here on earth is that it is preparation for our time in heaven. As Proverbs 11:4 tells us, "Wealth is worthless in the day of wrath, but righteousness delivers from death" (NIV). No matter how much money we have or don't have, what counts is how we treat others, not the treats we get for ourselves. Matthew 6:24 says, "No one can serve two masters. Either you will hate the one and love the other, or you will be devoted to the one and despise the other. You cannot serve both God and money" (NIV).

If Matthew were writing today, then he might also say that you cannot serve both God and your sports car, God and your timeshare, or even God and your child's Harvard education. All of these goods are great. They are the dessert of life, a nice treat. They are not the things you should be striving for.

Now, having said that money is not a good master, we will talk about how to be a good master of your money. First, you have to have faith that God will provide for your needs. In Philippians 4:19, we are told, "And my God will meet all your needs according to the riches of his glory in Christ Jesus" (NIV).

God put you on this earth. He will give you the tools you need to survive and take care of those you love. God is in a covenant with you. However, this fact does not mean that God is an ATM. He's not. You have to have faith in God, but you also have to have faith in yourself, in your abilities, in your talents. Now, having faith in these things does not mean what you might think it does. God gave you tools, but you have to learn how to use and keep them in good repair.

Does this concept of taking care of your tools sound familiar to you?

It should. It is the biblical concept of stewardship. We have to remember that we do not own anything at all. Even the things we think we own—our abilities and our skills—come from God. The Parable of the Talents encourages us to take care of our abilities, grow and employ them. In the Parable of the Talents (Matthew 25:14-30, ESV), Jesus tells us of a man who left his money in the keeping of several of his servants:

> For it will be like a man going on a journey, who called his servants and entrusted to them his property. To one he gave five talents, to another two, to another one, to each according to his ability. Then he went away. He who had received the five talents went at once and traded with them, and he made five talents more. So also he who had the two talents made two talents more. But he who had received the one talent went and dug in the ground and hid his master's money. Now after a long time the master of those servants came and settled accounts with them. And he who had received the five talents came forward, bringing five talents more, saying, "Master, you delivered to me five talents; here, I have made five talents more." His master said to him, "Well done, good and faithful servant. You have been faithful over a little; I will set you over much. Enter into the joy of your master." And he also who had the two talents came forward, saying, "Master, you delivered to me two talents; here, I have made two talents more.' His master said to him, 'Well done, good and faithful servant. You have been faithful over a little; I will set you over much. Enter into the joy of your master." He also who had received the one talent came forward, saying, "Master, I knew

> you to be a hard man, reaping where you did not sow, and gathering where you scattered no seed, so I was afraid, and I went and hid your talent in the ground. Here, you have what is yours." But his master answered him, "You wicked and slothful servant! You knew that I reap where I have not sown and gather where I scattered no seed? Then you ought to have invested my money with the bankers, and at my coming I should have received what was my own with interest. So take the talent from him and give it to him who has the ten talents. For to everyone who has will more be given, and he will have an abundance. But from the one who has not, even what he has will be taken away. And cast the worthless servant into the outer darkness. In that place there will be weeping and gnashing of teeth."

The message of the Parable of the Talents is clear: God gives us things. But at the end of our lives, God will want an accounting of what we did with what He gave us. Were we industrious? Did we get the proper education to get good employment and fully utilize our talents to benefit ourselves and others? On the flip side, did we spend our time flirting, drinking, playing on the internet, and having relationships—romantic or otherwise—with people we had no business being with? If we did not use our gifts to help others and ourselves, then we alone bear the consequences of our poor stewardship.

While it might not seem like it at certain times, God always keeps his covenant with us. In all realms—including finances, it is up to us to keep our covenant with Him.

Chapter 8

Intentionality

If stewardship is important in terms of talents and abilities, then it is also crucial in terms of managing money.

Here is a fact that may escape you when you are trying to pay the electric bill and are coming up short. During the course of their lifetimes, most people will earn well over a million dollars. For professionals such as doctors, lawyers, and some professors, that number could well be over two to five million dollars.

Yet, as we saw above, the American net worth is relatively low, retirement savings are practically non-existent, and over half the population could barely pay for a root canal if they needed one. Today, the average family is about $137,000 in debt. Some of that debt is mortgage debt because we all need a place to live (Federal Reserve, 2017). However, even mortgage debt is questionable. How many of us live in houses that are far bigger than what we need and are requiring us to carry mortgages that bring us to the brink of insolvency? The answer to both of these questions is, unfortunately, too many. God promised to provide for our needs, but He did not promise you a McMansion so that you could show off to the Joneses, whom you probably do not like anyway. Put a roof over the heads of your family, by all means. But while doing so, make sure you live within your means.

Apart from mortgage debt, most Americans have credit card debt of over $16,000, according to the Federal Reserve in 2017. With percentage rates upwards of twenty-nine percent—which would have been considered loansharking thirty years ago—credit cards threaten the financial well-being of many families. Now, I know that emergencies happen. They do. You must deal with them by any means necessary, including the use of credit cards. You might need to put an ER visit on the credit card. But do you need to put those new shoes that are much too expensive on the credit card? Do you need to put the family Red Lobster dinner that will not help your waistline anyway on the credit card? Do you need to put the charges for yet another dating service on the credit card?

You know the answer to these questions as well as I do. You do not need half of what you buy. God did not promise you any of these things—not even a subscription to *Christian Mingle*. But you might be thinking to yourself that you have to charge those Christmas and birthday gifts and those expensive vacations. You say this because you think your spouse and kids need good memories. They do. But what they do not need is to live in a household that teeters on the brink of financial ruin. You do not need that state of affairs, either.

What you all need is financial stability and memories produced not by products bought but by relationships enjoyed and time spent—not money spent.

So, how do you get this financial stability? You have to be incredibly intentional. You have to steward the money that God does send into your life. Although I am not Dave Ramsey, he is correct that sometimes it will have to be "beans and rice and rice and beans" until you get yourself on solid financial footing. While this may seem like it is going to be austere, budgeting and prioritizing your purchases is one of the most liberating things you can do for both yourself and your family.

How do you start? Be intentional. First, except for extreme emergencies, lay off the credit card. If you cannot pay for something in cash, then you cannot afford it. Second, get an emergency fund together. You are going to need it. Root canals and dead transmissions happen. Most financial experts agree that you need about 3-6 months of living expenses stashed. Third, start paying off those credit cards after you get your emergency fund established. Once you get those cards paid off, put them in a drawer and lock the drawer, or put them in a bag and freeze them. When you want to use them, you will have to let them thaw, and by then, the desire will have vanished.

Those are the basics. But even after you accomplish these tasks, you are far from being done. You need to plan for your future and the future of your family. This fact means that you need to start prioritizing. What is essential? Let's go with the basics. Current estimates are that a basic retirement will cost about $750,000, according to Merrill Lynch Finances in Retirement Survey in 2017. That figure does include money you will receive from Social Security—if it is still in existence in thirty years. You need to start planning for your future after work. Not tomorrow, not next week. Now. Ten to fifteen percent of your income should be saved for retirement. That number is a bare-bones minimum. Twenty percent would be better.

Next, your children's education is a priority. This does not mean that you have to send your child to an Ivy League school to be a good parent. If you are thinking about going this route, then know that the tuition for an Ivy League school like the University of Pennsylvania is over $71,000 a year. That is $280,000 for four years. Of course, colleges give scholarships. Still, even with aid packages, you might not be able to afford this kind of tuition—unless you are a high earner or have been saving since your child's conception. That is okay. State schools and community colleges do provide high-quality and reasonably priced education. Many agree that going to a state college is a better deal when comparing the education students receive.

It is not where you send your children to college. Rather, it is that you stress the importance of education and start preparing early for sending your kids to college. Not only does that mean saving, researching tuition prices, and using appropriate savings vehicles early on—it also means encouraging your kids to get good grades so that they have access to scholarship money. Education is a family effort from start to finish. Being intentional about homework results in good grades and leads to a family culture of attending college.

Finally, let's talk about the real purpose of money. First and foremost, you have to take care of the needs of you and your family. Notice I did not say wants. You have to be able to distinguish between needs and wants. Beyond taking care of your family's needs, you have to take care of your own. By your own needs, I mean the needs of your soul.

As I said above, money is a tool. One of its functions in the postmodern world is to help you to be generous. Tithe, give money to your church. Give money to your favorite charities. Give money to family members in trouble. A quick word of caution here: if you are going to help a family member or friend, then give money to them. Never lend it. Unpaid debts wreck even the strongest of relationships. Give if you want to, but do not expect anything back in this life. You will get your reward later. Give the money to extended family when they are in need and let it go.

Money and your attitude toward it are critical to your salvation. Just as you should spend your time developing yourself and serving others, you need to steward your money carefully and use it to help others and yourself.

The rewards of life are not monetary. The real rewards come at the end of life, not the beginning, and the biggest reward of all is the attainment of heaven. Remember, you cannot serve two masters. Make sure your family is intentional about that.

Serve the one who counts the most.

Intimacy

At first glance, money and intimacy might not seem to have much in common. That is only at first glance.

Intimacy and money go hand in hand in scripture. God expressed His need for intimacy through money. Malachi 3:7 says, "'Ever since the time of your ancestors you have turned away from my decrees and have not kept them. Return to me, and I will return to you,' says the LORD Almighty" (NIV). God says the Israelites left Him like a lover leaves their love. God says He knows they left Him because they no longer gave Him tithes. Jesus drives the point home further by saying, "For where your treasure is, there your heart will be also" (Matthew 6:21, NIV). God knew Israel's heart had left because He no longer saw their treasure. God wants intimacy, and one of the main things that stand in the way of that intimacy is our lack of tithing. When the family tithes, the family increases intimacy with God.

We live in a culture where there are four taboo topics: politics, religion, sex, and money. Money is on this list because money directly reflects our habits and even our identities. Think about how people speak: "He's worth four million. She's broke." Rightly or wrongly, our money is seen as defining who we are. Of course, who we are primarily is Christians.

As you can see in Malachi 3:7 and Matthew 6:21, intimacy and money have a lot to do with each other. If you and your spouse are not on the same page financially, then you will have a lot of trouble in the relationship. You could be a spender and your wife a saver. There is nothing wrong with this combination as long as you work together to develop a budget and agree on your priorities. Indeed, savers and spenders often go together. They are a complementary pair. Savers keep spenders from going broke, and spenders keep savers from becoming misanthropes and stingy misers.

The most important thing about money within a relationship is the most important thing about relationships in general: intimacy. There should be no secrets and no cheating. Make some time to sit down with your spouse at least once a week to talk about finances, go over bills, talk about credit card usage, discuss priorities about spending on yourself and your children, and track your progress on mortgage payments and retirement goals. As the family matures, make sure the children are a part of family financial discussions.

While a weekly finance date is not the most romantic or the sexiest way to spend an hour or so with your spouse, this is time well spent because it keeps the two of you from drifting apart financially. Since finances are the number one cause of divorce in the United States, this hour spent each week talking about finances is one of the best investments you can make in terms of your relationship with your spouse.

Remember, though, in these conversations, you should not be playing the blame game.

"You spent too much on a night out with the girls."

"You didn't really need those Broncos tickets. You should be out making more money, not having fun with the boys."

"Why did the kids need a hundred dollars for the weekend?"

Instead of blaming, stay focused on what is essential and how you will achieve your goals. Approach finances in the same manner that you should approach any topic that you raise with your spouse: with love and respect. The marriage counselor John Gottman has publicly said that almost all couples fight. That is normal behavior. But Gottman has said the difference between couples who stay together and those who divorce is that in their fights, the couples that eventually divorce show contempt for each other or try to shame each other. Nobody likes to be shamed or be shown contempt. Money is such a tricky subject that shame and contempt often come to the surface when tempers flare. Remember, your weekly meetings should be used to reach a consensus, not to attack your partner.

Intimacy with money should extend beyond you and your wife. Include your children in your weekly conversations once they are old enough to understand what you are talking about. Children need to see their parents talking about money in a respectful and sane way. Remember, how you are with money is how your children will be with money. They need to see you budgeting, spending for fun, saving, investing, and paying the bills.

Children also need to know what the family's financial priorities are. Your son may think that a Camaro is the biggest financial priority in the world. You need to explain to him that fancy sports cars are all well and good after you have dealt with bills, housing, and education. Your son may need wheels, but he might not need fancy wheels.

Indeed, one of the best things you can do for your children is to set up a joint savings account with them when they are about twelve or thirteen. If you give an allowance to your children, then teach your children the importance of both tithing and saving. Make your children tithe ten percent of their allowance and save ten percent. Financial habits are a lot like fitness habits. Just as children need to see their parents exercising and eating well, they also need to see their parents dealing responsibly with money.

While you should have family discussions about money and teach your children about saving and tithing, one thing you should not do is open a credit card account for them. Children do not need to learn how to use credit cards responsibly. They need to learn how to avoid the trap of credit altogether. If you get your teenager a credit card, then you are showing that child how to become addicted to credit. The best way to break a bad habit is never to start it in the first place.

Finally, as I said above, unpaid debt can wreck relationships. If your child asks you for money and you believe that they are asking you for a good reason, then by all means, give the child—or adult child—the money. However, you should never lend a child money beyond a couple of bucks. If the child does not pay the loan back, then you may resent the child, and the child may avoid you. You do not want either of those occurrences to happen.

In addition, we do live in a world where people get themselves in financial trouble. Because of these possibilities, you should never cosign on a loan with anyone except a mortgage loan with your spouse. Remember, you have to keep yourself strong to help other people. You cannot help others if your credit is destroyed because a child chose to be irresponsible in paying back a loan. The lender will come after you, and there can be dire consequences for you if you are responsible for someone else's loan.

So, talk about money with your spouse and children. This is one taboo that you absolutely should break for the sake of your family relationships and your children's futures.

Talk about money. It is important.

Empowerment

One has to be empowered with money. Now, empowerment can mean that you earn a lot. If you are a high-dollar earner, then that is great. You do have some power that others do not. Use that power responsibly. However, you do not have to be making six figures to be empowered with money.

The biggest thing you can do to improve your family's relationship with money is to pray. Pray for opportunities. Pray for guidance about how to be a good steward of your family's money. Pray for wisdom.

The second thing you can do is to develop a sense of mission around your money. What are you going to do with it? Once you answer that question, you can decide what you are not going to do with money. It is easy to say what you should not do with money—blow it on unimportant things that will not further your family's mission—but you have to have that financial mission clearly defined.

The third thing you can do to gain empowerment with your finances is to treat them like prayer and exercise—something you should be doing every day. Track your spending and set long-term savings goals. Some financial professionals say that you should track your net worth every ninety days. You should follow it every day. You should track your spending every day. Just as you are amazed by what thirty minutes of exercise a day can accomplish for your waistline, you will be surprised by what fifteen minutes a day of tracking spending and saving for your future can accomplish.

The story of Moses and the daughters of Zelophehad in Numbers 36:5-12 (NIV) is a great story of empowerment. It states:

> Then at the LORD's command Moses gave this order to the Israelites: "What the tribe of the descendants of Joseph is saying is right. This is what the LORD commands for Zelophehad's daughters: They may marry anyone they please as long as they marry within their father's tribal clan. No inheritance in Israel is to pass from one tribe to another, for every Israelite shall keep the tribal inheritance of their ancestors. Every daughter who inherits land in any Israelite tribe must marry someone in her father's tribal clan, so that every Israelite will possess the inheritance of their ancestors. No inheritance may pass from one tribe to another, for each Israelite tribe is to keep the land it inherits." So Zelophehad's daughters did as the LORD commanded Moses. Zelophehad's daughters—Mahlah, Tirzah, Hoglah, Milkah and Noah—married their cousins on their father's side. They married within the clans of the descendants of Manasseh son of Joseph, and their inheritance remained in their father's tribe and clan.

Moses empowered these women with God's commands. This was against all cultural moves, but God wanted to use money and inheritance to empower these daughters. God still overlooks and ignores cultural norms to empower families with an inheritance.

Learning from Life's Lessons

There is no more tenacious teacher of lessons learned than money. My family learned our lesson several years ago when I wanted to go into business. The opportunity to buy a bookstore came up. I saw dollar signs and easy money. How many of you know easy money is never easy?

Nevertheless, I pulled together some investors, and away we went to buy a bookstore and build a business. I found out quickly being a small business owner was a full-time job and then some. There was no time to plant a church and start a business. On top of that, I did not realize the book business was shifting from in-store buying to online purchases. We bought the bookstore at the worst possible time. Customers stayed away in droves. We made payroll. We paid our bills. We eventually paid our investors. But we lost hundreds of thousands of dollars.

Still, we learned a lesson. Easy money is never easy, and being a business owner requires hard work, homework, and capital. Money is a tenacious teacher and taskmaster. You cannot serve both mammon and God. One will ultimately be your master. Make sure it is God. All the other things will be added to you.

Ask God for help with your finances. The bank may turn you down, but God never will.

Reflection Questions

1. What are your family's financial goals?
2. Do you make it a goal to pray daily for financial wisdom?
3. How do you and your spouse talk about finances?
4. How have you stewarded the money that has come through your life?
5. How do you and your children talk about money?
6. If you and your spouse fight about money, then can you do so without showing contempt for each other?
7. How do you and your spouse serve as financial role models for your children?
8. Is it difficult for you to say "no" to a child's request for money for a purchase you think is unwise?
9. Do you tithe and give money to charities?
10. What is the most precious gift you can give your family?

Chapter 9

Military Families

Military families. They're unique.

Few families must endure what military families go through.

Sure, they struggle with the same things "normal" families do, such as making ends meet, arguing with a spouse, and disciplining unruly children. But with tension rising among the United States and countries overseas, military families undergo altogether unique stressors. Military members feel the strain of increased deployments to the Middle East, and the struggle to cope mounts with every deployment. The annual Blue Star Families Military Family Lifestyle survey revealed that the top five concerns among military members include job security, retirement benefits, financial security, and employment prospects for service members and their spouses. Not surprisingly, the fear of deployment overseas is the biggest source of family stress (*The Fiscal Times*, 2015).

The stress does not end when moving from active duty to retirement or civilian life. Veterans face a whole slew of unique family problems too. The Veterans Health Administration report in January 2014 revealed that the suicide rate among veterans and service members is higher than the national rate, with an estimated twenty-two veterans dying by suicide each day. Three out of five of these veterans were diagnosed with a mental health condition. Part of this comes from the traumatic events they witness while deployed. Injuries, grief, fear, sexual violence associated with combat, and repeated deployment and/or relocation takes a toll not only on service members, but their families as well. Add to that increased rates of substance abuse issues and high rates of homelessness, and you've got a recipe for disaster (SAMHSA, 2017).

Military service members have to serve themselves as they serve our nation. They are in a perpetual state of service. They are constantly in harm's way and are separated from their families for extended periods of time. Maintaining family life is a challenge and raising a fabulous family can seem like a pipe dream, but it is not. Military families have what it takes. I know because my family was a military family for twenty-one and a half years. I am a retired Air Force Chaplain Lieutenant Colonel. We moved sixteen times including in and out of base housing. I was deployed to Saudi Arabia twice. I had a remote assignment for one year without my family. We had our first child while I was on remote assignment to the Osan Air Base in South Korea. We lived in Germany for three years. For a brief moment we were even homeless when the owners of the house we lived in sold it out from under us with little to no notice. It was not easy.

I was passed over for promotion and then put on the fast track—my career had its ups and downs. There are few careers that can impact family development quite like military service. But with a little grace, intentionality, intimacy, empowerment, and learning from life's lessons, we were able to make it through as a fabulous family.

Your family can too.

Grace

A military family must have unconditional love for each other in order to weather the storms that family separations and constant moving can bring. Every time a military member is deployed it places enormous stress on the family. Inevitably, the car will break down, the toilet will stop up and flood the house, or a child will get sick. In our case, a child got sick.

Geoffrey II was less than a year old when I was deployed to Saudi Arabia, United Arab Emirates (UAE), and other undisclosed locations. My son was diagnosed with a hernia. Before I left, the doctor said if his hernia ever became strangulated, we would know by looking at him and he would need immediate attention. This was on top of his reflux condition which caused him to throw up his formula. But Geoffrey did not just throw up; he projectile vomited his formula across the room. This happened every time he had his bottle.

As soon I was settled into my deployment—you guessed it—his hernia became strangulated. The emergency room on the base did not recognize what was happening. He went from piercing cries to lifeless while Glenda held him in her arms. She pleaded with the intake technician to see him. She told the emergency room staff what the doctor told her. The more she talked, the more lifeless our baby boy became as his hernia became swollen. As is often the case, the spouse of the military member does not get the response that the military member wearing the rank would get. So, she waited in frustration and mounting fear as our son was literally dying in her arms.

It just so happened the new emergency room doctor, who had a permanent change of station to the base—often referred to as "PCS-ed" or "PCS-ing"—stopped by the emergency room to assess his new duty station. The doctor had just gotten off the highway. While looking around, he saw our son's chart. The doctor demanded to see him. The intake technician ran and got Glenda and our lifeless baby boy. After barely examining him, the new doctor yelled to staff: "Take this baby to the Regional Medical center off base immediately!" With tears in her eyes and fear in her heart, Glenda gave them our baby and followed the ambulance to the hospital. Friends followed her, other friends picked up our daughter Mahogany, and still other friends prayed. This was the military community support in action. The chapel family rose to the occasion. Everyone we knew was up-in-arms or on their knees in prayer.

Meanwhile, where was I?

I was sitting poolside at the luxury hotel of a secret location. I could not help that the outpost I was assigned to visit while deployed to Saudi Arabia was at a luxurious city. I could not help that the people I was supposed to minister to spent their off-duty time sitting by the pool ordering Arnold Palmers and making sure they ate the food per diem amount of fifty dollars a day. At this location, we were not allowed to wear our uniforms off the base. No one was supposed to know we were there. That was not my fault but I could not get Glenda to understand that. She was watching our son die without her husband. Anger and resentment crept into Glenda's heart. She had to pray for God's grace and agape love to help her get through the crisis and forgive me for I "knew not what I was doing."

Intentionality

I was not intentionally trying to exacerbate the situation, but there are times you have to be intentional if you want to grow up as a fabulous family in the military. A covenant family is intentional! Military life thrives in an intentional culture. Everything about military life is orderly, direct, and specific.

This culture of intentionality is also needed in family life because of the challenge military families face.

Stability is critical. We were separated for more than two years when I received orders to come to Scott Air Force Base in Illinois. My family chose to remain at our previous location, Langley Air Force Base in Virginia. We were conflicted as to whether I would continue my military career beyond twenty years or retire. Due to a variety of family issues—Mahogany in high school, Geoffrey II adapting to multiple moves—we desperately needed stability, which involved remaining intentional about every move I made. During that period, I was intentional about coming home every six weeks. I was intentional about putting together model planes with my son every time I came home. I was intentional about taking him to the movies. I was intentional about going to see my daughter as a drum major in her high school marching band. I was intentional about spending time with Glenda and making up for lost time. I was intentional about giving Glenda total control of the finances and allotting myself only twenty-five dollars per week. Times were tough and money was tight. Intentionality made all the difference. It was not just a matter of coming home regularly, but showing an interest in the activities my wife and children were involved in. It meant keeping up with their lives as much as I could, even if that required countless phone calls and trips back and forth.

One year, I had come home on a weekend—keeping with my intentional routine of coming home every six weeks. As was my practice, I preached at the chapel on Sunday morning before my flight home. My flight home departed that afternoon. There were several delays and connecting flight issues that almost left me stranded in Philadelphia. I barely made the last flight to Newport News, Virginia. Late that evening, a happy family picked me up at the airport. The house was full of joy because daddy was home for the week. It was September 10, 2001. The next day, I was awakened with the rest of the world to the 9/11 Attacks and the Twin Towers falling to the ground. My family was fearful, as was everyone's family. Glenda's job at one of the elementary schools sent the children home. We all huddled around the television wondering what happened and what was going to happen next. This time, I was with my family during the crisis—all because I had been intentional about coming home at regular intervals. I was not sitting by the pool sipping Arnold Palmers and talking on a satellite phone. I was home where I belonged. God kept us together through fearful times. He will keep your family together, too, as long as you stay intentional about your actions and how they affect the family.

Empowerment

Military families must be families of empowerment or they will not survive. A covenant family must be in the empowerment zone at all times. Every family member must empower one another to succeed. Empowerment requires trust in one another and trust in God. Our empowerment zone was created early on in our family. It is something you should establish early on in your family, too.

My first permanent change of station was during our first pregnancy. The problem was, I was PCS-ing to Osan Air Base in South Korea and Glenda was going to our follow-on assignment at Langley Air Force Base in Virginia. We lived there twice. This was the first time. We were young and ignorant to the ways of the military. We were still just learning how to be married. Now, our first big move from New York to Virginia was followed by my PCS to South Korea a week later.

Glenda was three months pregnant in a city she had never lived in before. We knew no one. This was before cell phones, FaceTime, email, social media, and the internet. She was just as remote as I was. As an officer, I did not get free morale calls and the Korean phone system left much to be desired. All we had was God, letters, and an occasional base operator connection to my home phone. I was slated to go home for my mid-tour leave just in time for our special delivery. But, you guessed it—Mahogany came early. Glenda had to go to the hospital and deliver by herself. She felt empowered to do so because we had prayed without fail every day. God heard our prayers.

When Glenda went into labor, I felt a pain way in South Korea. I asked the base operator to connect me. I knew Glenda had gone into labor. I just knew it. Six hours later with me on the phone, she delivered a healthy baby girl. Her empowerment came from God. He blessed us by allowing me to be on the phone with her through the delivery.

There may be times your family goes through something similar, with one spouse deployed. It might not be the delivery of a baby but another family circumstance. Even something as small as a parent-teacher conference requires the empowerment of one spouse to another. Sometimes simply ensuring your spouse you recognize and appreciate the work they are putting in each day to head the household and act as the only parent in the house is enough. And vice versa. Letting your deployed spouse know you are proud of them and their service gives them the recognition they need to continue on in times of difficulty and stress.

Chapter 9

Intimacy

Someone once said intimacy could be referred to as "into me you see." Intimacy is too commonly thought of as sexual. This thinking prevents real intimacy between relationships and in particular, family relationships. Covenant families have a deep desire to become intimate—breaking down barriers that prevent family members from seeing the needs and personhood of each other.

Intimacy takes time. Intimacy takes care. Intimacy requires patience. Intimacy means putting aside social media, turning off the television, and spending time with each other.

Military families have more time together when they learn to reframe their situation. Because military families are always relocating—in our case, sixteen times—making new relationships outside of the family is difficult. The constant is the relationships built within the family. The constant moving requires families to get to know one another because they are the only ones you know for much of the time in your military career.

My family and I really got to know one another when we moved to Germany. We lived in one of the villages near the base. Our children did not have the benefit of having friends in the stairwell housing on base. They could not walk to the youth center and make friends. Neither could they speak the language of the German children in the village we lived in. They had each other, Glenda, and me as playmates.

We started Friday night family nights. After chapel on Sundays, we ate dinner and fell asleep on our bed watching NFL football over the Armed Forces television network. We rode our bikes through the village. We took family walks and looked at the date inscriptions on the village houses. To our surprise, some of the houses were older than America. We spent time together making pizza and learning about the Bible through family Bible study and videos. We talked to each other. That's right. We talked. These intimate moments turned into days and weeks, and our routine benefited us at our next duty station. Into each other we see!

My next assignment was the Air Force Institute of Technology at the University of Memphis. I was sent there to get my crisis intervention counseling education specialist degree. I had civilian status for a year living in the suburbs of Memphis, Tennessee without a base community to attach to. No chapel community. No base housing. No military culture. The only people we knew were each other, so we were applying what we learned in Germany. Our children were the new, strange kids in school. "Military brats," they called them. We had to turn up the volume—spend even more time together. For me, it was easier because all I had to do was go to class, study, and write papers. But our budget was tight. We had gotten used to all the extra allowances living in Germany had brought. Now all of that was gone, so we had to make do. We went to the cheapest fast food places we could find and had Friday nights at Sonic. We played board games. We made it work. Into each other we see!

These lessons proved priceless as my next assignment was a staff job in the Washington, D.C. area. Again, no base. No chapel. Thankfully, there were plenty of other military and government "brats" in the neighborhood. At that time, we were coasting because we had become such a close-knit family. We learned how to be intimate; your family can do the same. Spend time together. Figure out what everyone likes. Develop a strong sense of intimacy and you will be able to sail through any difficulty as a fabulous family in covenant with each other. Into each other we see!

Learning from Life's Lessons

There are a lot of lessons learned from being a military family that other families can benefit from. Many are beyond the scope of this book—but when you sum them up and put them in the form of orders, to use a little bit of military language—then they would boil down to doing two things. Both stem from military jargon. The Air Force has a saying: "Flexibility is the key to air power." The Army has a saying, "Adapt and overcome." Both apply when it comes down to a military family. In fact, all families can learn from these two sayings.

The key to staying strong and fabulous when your family is bouncing all around the country—and sometimes around the world—is flexibility. You must learn how to be flexible. Flexibility is indeed the key to overpowering the many challenges constant moving brings. Each part of the country has a way of doing things. Each utility company, apartment complex, and school has its way of completing registration, deposits, and cutoff notices. Insisting on your way will only frustrate each move and add to the stress of your family moving every few years. This flexibility lends itself to application in everyday family life. You have to learn to be flexible with new friends, new routines, and even new weather climates. Once flexibility becomes the culture of your family, it finds its way into solving family problems.

As a fabulous military family, you must also adapt and overcome, as the Army says. It sounds similar to "Flexibility is the key to air power," but it is not. When the Army uses that phrase, they are talking about not being overwhelmed by problems that could endanger advancing the troops to victory. Every family can be victorious in the Lord, especially if they remember Satan works overtime to defeat families. John 10:10 says, "The thief comes only to steal and kill and destroy; I have come that they may have life, and have it to the full" (NIV). As a military family, separation and a spouse constantly in harm's way is always a threat to abundant life. How does the family adapt and overcome? A family can overcome by faith and not by sight, as 2 Corinthians 5:7 says. And remember what 2 Timothy 1:7 says: "For the Spirit God gave us does not make us timid [fearful], but gives us power, love and self-discipline" (NIV).

Finally, know that even though you may walk through the valley of the shadow of death—i.e. constant deployments to Afghanistan, Iraq, and other places to defend our country—God will make a table before you in the presence of your enemies (Psalm 23:4). Goodness and mercy shall follow your family all the days of their lives as they adapt and overcome the challenges of being a military family. In fact, these lessons learned are applicable to all families. Faith in God is the best remedy and strategy to applying the Air Force adage, "Flexibility is the key to your success."

Chapter 9

Reflection Questions

1. What is the top stressor in your military family? How does your family work together to make sure it does not tear the family apart?
2. How do you use grace in your family? How do you demonstrate grace to the other military families around you?
3. Is your family stable? How can you establish stability?
4. Do you practice intentionality in your family? How?
5. What does your family's empowerment zone look like?
6. How can you empower your military family when they are feeling the stress of a deployed family member?
7. How can you reframe your military family's situation to create intimacy?
8. Why is intimacy an important part of a fabulous military family?
9. How does your family embody the military phrase, "Flexibility is the key to air power"?
10. How does your family "adapt and overcome"?

Chapter 10

Same-Sex Families

One may ask why a book on family based in a faith tradition includes a chapter on same-sex families. Great question! According to estimates from the 2019 Current Population Survey Annual Social and Economic Supplement (CPS ASEC), 543,000 same-sex married couple households and 469,000 households with same-sex unmarried partners live together. There are estimates of 230,000 same-sex families within the Body of Christ. To think that by not talking about them, they would somehow disappear or go away is a mistake we often make in the Body of Christ. Ignoring an issue does not make it dissipate.

In some cases, ignoring an issue can make it grow even more in stature and influence. So it has been in America. Same-sex marriage has issues with theology, church, state, and society, that have grabbed national headlines, in part because of the church's inadequate compassionate response. In June 2015, the Supreme Court issued its *Obergefell v. Hodges* decision, which ruled that states must allow same-sex couples to marry. A Pew Forum poll before the decision found that most Americans (57%) thought same-sex marriage should be legal, but less than a third of evangelicals, word and faith churches, holiness, Pentecostal, and most mainline churches agreed. This did not stem the tide.

Same-sex families have slowly become a part of the culture. The normalization of same-sex families has happened without consultation nor consent from the community of the Body of Christ. As opinions are formed, the Body of Christ must have an informed theological idea about any high-profile volatile issues in the culture. It does not mean the informed opinions will rule the day. It does mean the culture would have heard the unified voice of the Body of Christ that is not strident and shrill but well-reasoned.

Perhaps some would be influenced by Paul, who said the gospel would be advanced irrespective of the situation the gospel is found in (Philippians 1:2). What is the theological position that needs to be heard in the marketplace? Same-sex families are recipients of God's grace like all other families. Same-sex families also want to raise a covenant fabulous family. Same-sex families have the same aspirations for their children as every other family does in the Body of Christ. To speak to this does not mean one embraces the sin, but neither does addressing all other families mean embracing their sins.

In this chapter, you will stand outside the closed door of the closet that a same-sex family has been outside of for the better part of their lives. They are members of my church. You will read their candor about the five principles all the other families deal with. They agreed to share their family story. Their honesty will challenge you, as it did me. It will also allow you to step out of your place of judgment and possibly learn what you never thought possible: God's grace is for everyone.

Grace

Alice and Sally (aliases) have been married for several years. After the Supreme Court decision, they traveled to a state that had passed laws giving them the right to marry. They had met at a party and were attracted to each other from the outset. Both were already public with their sexuality. Each already had children. Sally was previously married in a heterosexual relationship. She was forward about her sexuality. Sally believes God's grace covers her because she believes that she was born homosexual. Sally's words are, "You might be surprised who shows up in heaven." She goes on to say, "I am very comfortable in my skin, by God's grace. Whether others are or not is not my cross to bear."

Alice was equally open about her sexuality and God's grace. Alice grew up in the church. She was a preacher's kid—a "PK." She had not been inside a church in a long time until joining New Life. She said that since a church leader raped her, it has been challenging to go back inside any church. She has wrestled with why the church did not hold the person accountable. Given their experiences, I asked why they chose New Life.

They chose New Life after searching for a church when they relocated to the area. They attended other churches but did not feel God's grace. Their first visit to New Life was filled with acceptance, but my sermon gave them power. They returned because their children enjoyed the children's ministry. After the next visit, they both agreed that the grace and love were real. They did not decide where they would go to church based on whether the church accepts their sexuality or marriage. They both were raised in the church and wanted their children to be raised in the church, too. These decisions provided the church with the opportunity to extend grace to their children. Their children faithfully attended our Kids Rock children's ministry. Their children gave their lives to Christ and were baptized at New Life. Alice and Sally were attracted to the grace of Christ represented at New Life, in part because of the next principle of a fabulous covenant family: intentionality.

Intentionality

Alice and Sally are intentional about their family life. They were intentional about picking a church. They expressed how intentional they are when it comes to their sexuality. They discussed their sexuality with their children and told them they had two mommies. Their grade school children accept their two mothers. Alice and Sally also are intentional about their interactions with others. If you do not accept them, then they are not bothered nor discouraged. They say the person that does not accept them does not determine their standing before God.

They were intentional about roles in their family life. In particular, Sally firmly pushed back at the idea one of them should be the "man" as leader of the family and the other the domicile woman. She explained, "Whoever gets home first cooks, and everybody cleans." Do not try to boss her around by taking on the male leadership role. Their intentionality was self-evident in our more-than-an-hour interview.

Intimacy

One would think creating intimacy in a same-sex relationship would be an awkward topic. Not for Alice and Sally. To create intimacy, one must create a safe space. Trust must be paramount. Violation of that trust will hamper intimacy. Alice and Sally were struggling with intimacy. They were struggling with trust. Infidelity had twice crept into their marriage. It was clear the wounds had not healed. Alice had not been faithful.

They openly discussed her cheating and lies to cover it up. Sally was clear the relationship "is not a baseball game." She was not willing to give another hit at-bat. The tension and lack of trust were palpable. Same-sex couples struggle with intimacy just like heterosexual couples. They both agreed they were back on the road to intimacy, but it was hard.

Empowerment

Both Alice and Sally exhibited a tremendous amount of empowerment. Sally told me that one of her sons is gay. She shared his struggle and coming out as gay. She said she did not encourage him either way. She empowered him to decide if he felt he was born gay. One would think she would have pushed him into it. Sally was clear this was something between him and God. Both Alice and Sally were committed to their children spending time with their biological fathers. They said, "Our being gay doesn't mean they don't have fathers." Their grade school children spend summers with their fathers. The children of Alice and Sally have been empowered to travel the road to discovery of who they are.

Learning from Life's Lessons

When asked what lessons would be learned in a same-sex marriage family, Alice and Sally talked about creating trust and increasing faith. Isn't it interesting that faith in each other and God was the lesson learned that they wanted others to know about?

Upon reflection about the same-sex family being in covenant in having a fabulous family, I see that they can understand it for themselves. Alice and Sally were not ashamed of their family. They were empowered to be a fabulous family, whether I agreed with them or not. I welcomed their story. Their voice was heard—not to counter scripture—but to broaden who we will invite into the house of God. I could not, nor did I, reject them access to God's house. Rejecting them is not my job. God has the final say. He told me to go out into the highways and byways to compel men and women to come into His house, and it would be filled. He said the separation of sheep and goats would come at the end done by Him, not me (Matthew 25: 31-33). Alice, Sally, and their children made it easy. They accepted us before we accepted them. Now that is grace. That is a covenant church family.

Resources:

https://www.census.gov/newsroom/press-releases/2019/same-sex-households.html

https://www.christianitytoday.com/ct/topics/s/same-sex-marriage/

Chapter 11

African American Families: *The History and Resilience*

We have almost reached the end of the book but not the story of the covenant family. We will end with a special discussion of the unique challenges faced by the African American family in the United States.

All ethnic and class groups—except for maybe some white, ethnic English, ruling-class families—have experienced harsh discrimination and hatred in the United States. In the nineteenth century, Irish, Italian, and Jewish immigrants were often beaten and killed. In the twentieth century, immigrant groups from Asia and Latin America experienced discrimination and hatred, too. While the United States is a melting pot, all of those sailing past Lady Liberty in New York have experienced rough times. The melting pot has some scorched vegetables at the bottom.

That said, African Americans have a unique history. Unlike any other ethnic group, African Americans spent over three hundred years as slaves in the United States. African Americans were brought here in chains through the Middle Passage for one purpose: to work the land and build this country without reward. From the discovery of America to the Emancipation Proclamation, the African American experience in the United States was primarily forced labor and slavery. History makes African Americans' experiences different than other groups. No other ethnic group can make that claim, nor would they want to.

Most of the founders of the United States, including Thomas Jefferson, owned slaves. The founders failed to recognize the intellectual incompatibility of the fundamental equality of human beings with chattel slavery. The truth is that slavery was part of the North American economy for three centuries. It is not easy to change an entire mode of economic production. However, that change took place through one of the bloodiest conflicts in U.S. history, the American Civil War.

Race-based slavery in the United States ended in 1865 with the Thirteenth Amendment to the United States Constitution and the defeat of the Confederacy by the Union Army. However, just because Lee handed his sword to Grant at Appomattox Courthouse and a piece of paper was signed by Congress in Washington does not mean that three hundred years of bigotry, injustice, discrimination, and self-hatred were wiped out.

They were not.

To understand the problems of the African American family in the twenty-first century, we need to take a look at the history of them from their roots in Africa through slavery, the Civil War, Jim Crow, the Civil Rights era, and our own supposedly race-blind era, which is anything but blind to race.

While the start of the modern era in the fifteenth century featured the development of science and technology, the

European settlement of the Americas, navigation of the world, and the eventual invention of human rights in the eighteenth century, the era also featured the destruction of much of African civilization. Two developments marked the beginning of this destruction. The first was the modern conception of race. Before the fifteenth century, race as we know it did not exist as a category. There were lighter-skinned people and darker-skinned people. But in the fifteenth and following centuries, Europeans landed in the Americas. They had to justify both the destruction of native peoples and the use of Africans as free labor in the New World. The irony is that while the Europeans tried to use natives as slave labor, many of these natives succumbed to European diseases and did not prove suitable slaves. Thus, Europeans turned to Africa to quench their thirst for free labor.

When an expansionist society with no regard for other cultures encounters a relatively different civilization, the historical results are usually disastrous for the civilization without weaponry or self-determination. While Columbus did sail the ocean blue in 1492, the age of exploration created havoc in Africa. From 1525 to approximately 1866, 12.5 million Africans were transported to the New World in slave ships. About 10.7 million survived the Middle Passage and became enslaved in the Americas (Trans-Atlantic Slave Trade Database). We will look at the impact of this cultural disaster on the African American family in a bit.

Before we do that, though, we cannot understand the contemporary African American family without understanding that the African family structure has always been different from that of the European nuclear family.

Chapter 11

The Traditional African Family

While it is not proper to talk about the "African" family any more than it is to talk about "European" culture since both continents hosted and continue to host a diversity of cultures, we can make a few generalizations about families in Africa. Before the arrival of the Europeans on the continent, the traditional African family differed radically from the family structure in Christendom. The African family can be defined in terms of three features: polygamy, matrilineal families, and extended families.

Technically speaking, many African cultures featured polygamy, the marriage of one man to two or more wives. However, the practice of polygamy required wealth. It was not easy to support two wives; thus, most men did not have more than one wife.

Another essential aspect of African families was extended kinship. For example, most of the Bantu peoples of Central and Southern Africa, Zimbabwe, South Africa, and Zambia had—and continue to have—extended families. In these families, brothers of the father are called "father," sisters of the mother are called "mother," and all children, known to our culture as cousins, are called "brother." This trait is the dominant essence of African American families today. In this kind of family, all children relate to the extended family, the "clan," more than they do to the nuclear family. Hence, Big Mama, play cousins, church mothers, TT, and so on.

Among some African peoples—especially the Bemba of Zambia—marriage is "matrilocal," which means that men go to live with their wives. As is the case with other African families, the extended family, rather than the nuclear family, composed the base unit of society. In the Bemba as well, the family is matrilineal; kinship based on the female line.

These three qualities—multiple partners, extended families, and matrilineal descent—will play themselves out in the contemporary African American family ("The Traditional African Family," Tembo, 2017).

The African American Family and Slavery

Before we go to the present, we must talk about the horrors of slavery. The African diaspora—in which over 10 million Africans were brought to the Americas in chains—wreaked havoc on families.

Prior to the diaspora, most Africans were not Christian. Christianity during the slave era was a double-edged sword for African Americans. On the one hand, Christianity was the religion of white elites and owners who used their versions of Christianity to enslave Africans further. Of course, both Old Testament and New Testament societies owned slaves. So, the Bible, to some extent, justified slavery. In addition, modern notions of racism often found justification in the Hamitic Hypothesis, or "Curse," which said that Africans were the descendants of Ham, a son of Noah. According to the Bible, Ham dishonored Noah, who cursed Ham's youngest son, Canaan. Although now thoroughly discredited, the Curse of Ham was used by European Christians and the church to justify slavery (*"The Hamitic Hypothesis; Its Origin and Functions in Time Perspective,"* Sanders, 2014).

The curse aside, Christianity also benefited African Americans in many ways. First and obviously, African Americans could use the Bible's story in Exodus of the enslavement of the Israelites by Egyptians to frame their own experience of slavery. The scriptures also show that God was always on the side of the oppressed. They saw Jesus raised from the dead, and therefore there was hope. Second, Christ's teachings inspired abolitionists in the nineteenth century to work to end slavery.

Family life for African Americans during slavery in the United States was routine in many ways and not common in others. As Harriet Beecher Stowe shows in *Uncle Tom's Cabin*, many slaves were Christianized by their masters and encouraged to develop their own families. The trouble, of course, was that at any moment, African American families could be broken up because of the owner's need to sell slaves—similar to how today we might need to sell assets to cover a financial emergency. The result of the commodification of human beings destroyed families.

A remarkable project of the Roosevelt-era Works Project Administration in the 1930s featured interviews with former slaves. These interviews confirm the damage that slavery did to the family structure of African Americans. One can see the destruction and hear the anguish in this account of former slave Sarah Graves:

> I am goin'' on 88 years right now (1937). I was brought to Missouri when I was six months old, along with my mama, who was a slave owned by a man named Shaw. We left my papa in Kentucky, 'cause he was allotted to another man. My papa never knew where my mama went, an' my mama never knew where papa went. They never wanted mama to know, 'cause they knowed she would never marry so long she knew

> where he was. Our master wanted her to marry again and raise more children to be slaves. Mama said she would never marry again to have children. So she married my step-father, Tattle Barber, 'cause he was sick an' could never be a father. He was so sick he couldn't work, so me and mama had to work hard. (*Federal Writers' Project: Slave Narrative Project, Vol. 10*, Missouri, Abbot-Younger, 1936).

Imagine never knowing your father or that your mother is seen simply as breeding stock. Another former slave, Silas Dothrum, said:

> I don't know where I was born and I don't know when. I know I am eighty-two or eighty-three years old. The white folks that raised me told me how old I was. I never saw my father and my mother in my life. I don't know nothin'. I'm just an old green man. I don't know none of my kin people—father, mother, uncles, cousins, nothin'. When I found myself the white people had me. (*Slave Narratives: A Folk History of Slavery in the United States from Interviews with Former Slaves: Volume II, Arkansas Narratives, Part 2*, 2014).

This man had no family life at all. Slavery completely unmoored him as a child from anybody who could have loved him. Imagine what that lack of close bonding does to a person.

Before we move on, let's hear from one last former slave to fully understand what slavery did to our people in the United States:

> My name is John W. Fields and I'm eighty-nine years old. I was born March 27, 1848 in Owensburg, KY. That's 115 miles below Louisville, KY. There was 11 other children besides myself in my family. When I was six years old, all of us children were taken from my parents, because my master died and his estate had to be settled. We slaves were divided by this method. Three disinterested persons were chosen to come to the plantation and together they wrote the names of the different heirs on a few slips of paper. These slips were put in a hat and passed among us slaves. Each one took a slip and the name on the slip was the new owner. I happened to draw the name of a relative of my master who was a widow. I can't describe the heartbreak and horror of that separation. I was only six years old and it was the last time I ever saw my mother for longer than one night. Twelve children taken from my mother in one day. Five sisters and two brothers went to Charleston, Virginia, one brother and one sister went to Lexington, KY, one sister went to Hartford, KY, and one brother and myself stayed in Owensburg, KY. My mother was later allowed to visit among us children for one week each year, so she could only remain a short time at each place. (*W.P.A. Slave Narratives, Federal Writers' Project*, 2007).

People wonder why there is dysfunction in the African American family, why out-of-wedlock births happen, and why there is despondency. Yes, it has been over 150 years since the abolition of slavery, but that time is only half of a three-hundred-year period. Time may heal all wounds, but the wounds inflicted upon African Americans, as John

Fields demonstrates, are deep. The disintegration of the African American family is still harvesting dysfunction and fractionation.

My Slave History – Mother's Side (The Best Family Lineage)

All African American families have their own stories. I recently commissioned the professional genealogists at *Ancestry* to research my family's beginnings. What I learned was not surprising. My great-great-grandfather on my mother's side, Willis, and his wife Annica were slaves in Wayne County, North Carolina. Probate court records confirm that they were treated as pieces of property to be divided amongst white heirs of Tuesday Theophilus W. Best.

Black people—evidenced by the treatment of Willis and Annica—were historically treated no differently than a plow, horse, or piece of land in the eyes of the law. There was no humanity, and certainly nothing godly, about how black slaves were treated by Christian white people.

Richard Best, the white man who inherited Willis, embraced slavery so much that he fought and died in the Civil War to retain the right to *own* black people. Although *Ancestry* could first confirm Willis as a freeman in 1870, the actual dates of his enslavement are unknown. Still, the effects of his enslavement have shaped the evolution of my family for five generations.

Consider my maternal grandmother, Minnie Best, born in Goldsboro, Wayne County, North Carolina, and died July 12, 1999. She was the daughter of Isaac Best and Ida "Minnie" Armstrong. Isaac Best died when Minnie was a child. Minnie's mother Ida died on July 11, 1957. Ida was the daughter of Jason Armstrong and Sarah Bunn.

Isaac Best probably died somewhere around 1909 or 1910. He certainly died before the 1910 Federal Census was enumerated because Ida appears as a widow and the head of her household. Ida's children, Willie, Wanneta [sic], Elijah, Minnie, Sarah, and her stepson, Joe I. Best, were also living with her. The 1880 Census shows Isaac was the son of Willis and Anarky [sic] Best. At that time, Isaac was 14 years old. Stepping back ten years to the 1870 census reveals the Best family living in New Hope Township of Wayne County. Isaac was four years old. His mother's name was spelled as "Anica." Living with or right next to Willis Best's family was 21-year-old Luke Best and his 67-year-old mother, Zilpha Best.

One vital record, found by *Ancestry.com*, revealed Willis and Anica Best's marriage was registered in Wayne County on August 4, 1866. At that time, formerly enslaved couples who had not been legally married could declare their union so that it could be recognized as a valid marriage by the state. Willis and "Anakey" [sic] stated they had resided together as man and wife for fifteen years, which means they started their union around 1851. The most important clue obtained from this record was that Anica's maiden surname was also "Best." The fact she and Willis had lived together since 1851 as a couple suggested that they either came from the same plantation or plantations geographically close together. Their union would have also likely been sanctioned by their former slaveholder.

Records suggest that the slaveholder was Theophilus W. Best. Several members of the Willis and Anica Best family are buried in the Theophilus W. Best family cemetery. Theophilus W.

Best was a white, documented former slaveholder in Wayne County. Theophilus W. Best died in 1857. His estate was administered by the Wayne County Probate Court between the years 1857 and 1859. The estate inventory first mentioned these enslaved persons on December 29, 1857. The list of slaves included Willis and Zilpha.

As the probate process progressed, Theophilus W. Best's property, which included his land and the list of enslaved persons on the estate, was divided into 12 equal lots—one for each of his heirs ("Best & Armstrong Families," *AncestryProGenealogists Research* Report, May 2021). The heirs then drew straws to determine who would inherit which lot. Estate divisions like this were often how enslaved families were split and divided. Slaves were assigned a dollar value like any other piece of property. The division of slaves was then arranged in "equal shares" to be divided amongst the heirs. The final estate division took place two years after Theophilus W. Best's death.

For enslaved people, waiting for news of final probate arrangements was usually a stressful and challenging time. The enslaved persons had no say where they would end up. One can only imagine how difficult and heart-wrenching the experience of being separated from their family must have been. Willis Best experienced this firsthand. He was placed in a lot drawn by Theophilus's daughter Mary (Best) Phillips. Zilpha and Luke were placed into separate lots. There are likely other biological family members who were separated, although records are incomplete. It is important to note that neither Willis's wife, Anica, nor any of their children were named in the Probate court documents of Theophilus W. Best. This fact indicates they were living on a different plantation—possibly another Best related to Theophilus.

Regardless, we know that the enslavement of Willis and Anica tore apart their family.

The white Best family settled in the Wayne County area in the early 1700s. Several generations of large families meant there were many slaveholding Bests in the region. The size of the problem of the white Best family is exponentially large for the African American Community. There is no doubt, based on the Wayne County Probate Court records, the white Best family enslaved many African Americans, which included the inhumanity of ripping families apart. The effects of the white Best family's dehumanizing of their slaves are visible in all of the social ills plaguing generations of African American families.

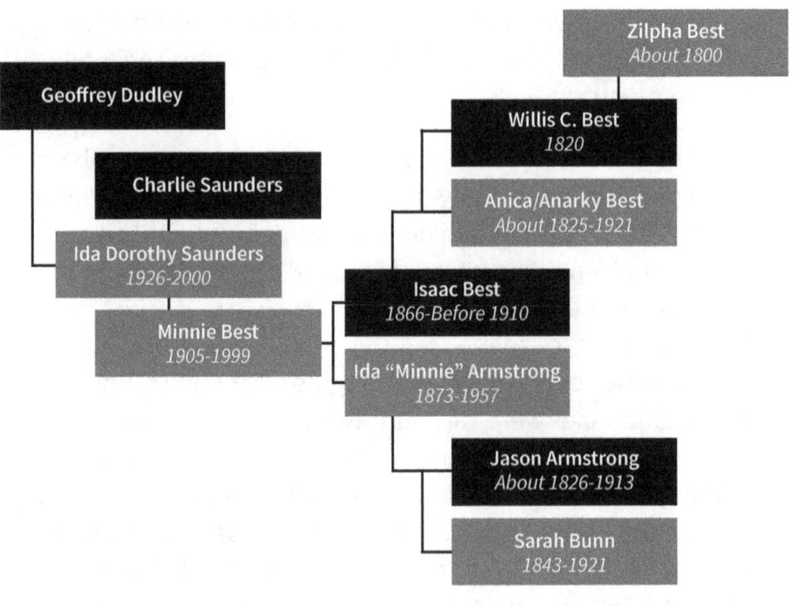

My Slave History – Father's Side (The Dudley Lineage)

My great-grandfather on my father's side, Daniel Dudley, was born in North Carolina in 1880 to James and Nicey Dudley. Daniel had a wife, Nettie, and sons Gaston, Jasper, and James. He died in 1936 at the age of 56. James and Nicey lived in Wayne County, North Carolina, and records list that they had two daughters who never appeared on the census again—they may have died young.

In 1870, James and Nicey Dudley lived on Willis Cole's plantation. Willis Cole owned slaves before the Civil War. Marriage records have led to the connection of another slave owner. It is uncertain whether or not Willis Cole owned James Dudley prior to the Civil War. Because records were not well kept for slaves, we cannot definitively state by whom my ancestors were enslaved. Many times, slaves took the surnames of plantation owners, but there does not appear to be any white slave-owning Dudleys during that time. Therefore, the conclusion is that James Dudley was most certainly born into slavery. The clear conclusion for me is that both sides of my family came to the United States in chains, enslaved to white so-called Christians.

Knowing about the slave owner is vital in compiling African American research. Researchers often look to the census in 1870, as this is the first time emancipated slaves appear at the end of the Civil War. Slaves often stayed in the same area where they had lived on plantations; some of them even stayed in the exact location after the war working for the same white families they had previously been enslaved by. This suggests that the Dudleys remained in the Wayne County area.

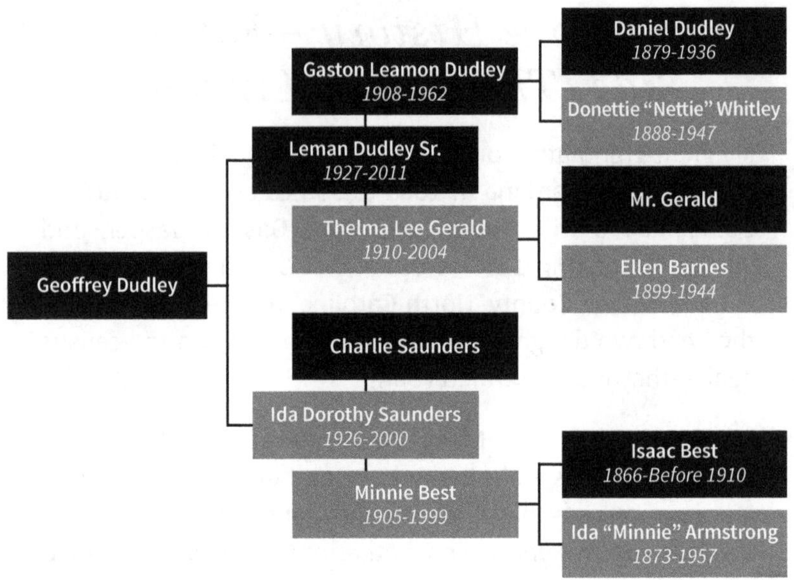

Post-Civil War

Just as Israel was led out of slavery by Moses, so too were African Americans freed through the efforts of abolitionists, the Union Army, and the creators of the Thirteenth Amendment. But, as I said above, the surrender of Lee and the signing of the Thirteenth Amendment were not enough to end three centuries of bigotry and hatred.

After the Civil War, African Americans were allowed to have families whose solidity did not depend on the economic fortunes of owners. However, as we all know, the attempts by the Republicans to reconstruct the South did not end well. After the Union army pulled out of the former Confederacy in 1876, the South returned to business as usual. Slavery was illegal in name. But that fact did not mean that African

Americans were not discriminated against by those who wanted to keep them down and oppressed.

At a core level, things did improve in that mothers did not have to see husbands and children sold down the river. Yet, how healthy could our families be when we were lynched by the thousands, our churches burned, and our fates decided by people who hated us?

The post-Civil War period saw the development of the Ku Klux Klan, Jim Crow laws, and racist customs. White men could call grown black adults by their first name, but those same adults were treated like children and had to call whites "Mr." Equality was a pipe dream. We could not use the same bathrooms, ride in the same trains, nor send our children to the same schools as whites. What do you think that did to our children? What do you think that did to our families? What do you think that did to our lives? It taught us internalized self-hatred manifested in what we wear, how we style our hair, and how we treat and mistreat each other.

As families, we could and did stick together maybe precisely because we had not previously been able to do so. Our nuclear families were strong, and the churches provided the strength, a bedrock of faith. We stuck together through hatred, church burnings, lynchings, snubs, and denial of basic human rights. We stuck together through the lack of an ability to use the same bathroom, get a sandwich at a lunch counter, stay in a nice hotel, or enjoy a comfortable seat on a train or bus. For almost a hundred years—from the departure of the Union Army from the South in 1876 through the signing of the Civil Rights Act in 1964—we had strong families, extended and otherwise, maybe only because we needed them desperately.

Chapter 11

The Civil Rights Era

As we all know, the United States was on fire in the 1960s. The war in Vietnam consumed lives—black and white. Militant activist groups of all flavors and races wanted to change the country radically.

Change did happen. Now, don't get me wrong: some of this change was good. The work of people like Dr. Martin Luther King, Jr., whose civil disobedience was divinely inspired by the Sermon on the Mount, helped people to begin to obtain the economic and racial justice they so deserved. In addition to the civil rights and protest movements, the Great Society programs of President Johnson declared war on poverty. Affirmative Action and the Civil Rights Act helped African Americans to gain admission to universities and professional schools. We were able to move forward and begin to claim our rights as American citizens.

But do you know what? The sixties were a mixed bag in terms of the African American family. On one level, blacks began to experience less overt discrimination, especially at the institutional level. On the other hand, doors opened, and that opening was good. Still, other parts of the sixties were awful for the African American family. The sixties featured protest movements against the war and racism, the beginning of Postmodern Thought, liberal whites becoming sensitized to our cause, and the sometimes over-reliance on social and economic welfare programs.

I saw some of this sympathy myself as a second-grader. There were eleven children in my family. We were poor, so when I complained of a stomachache, home remedies were the solution. After the baking soda water, ginger ale, cold compress, and milk and crackers all failed to work, my parents took me to the doctor. After examining me, I remember the doctor's words to my parents as if it were yesterday: "Take him to the hospital immediately!" he exclaimed. It turns out my appendix had ruptured, and the resulting poison was in my system for over a week. I had to have an emergency appendectomy. The next thing I remember was waking up in a hospital room. I had an open incision. I had to sleep upright so the pus from the rupture could drain out. I stayed in the hospital for three weeks. I remember getting a lot of visitors, but the visit from my second-grade teacher was the one that stood out the most. When Mrs. Bowden came to see me, it was as if an angel had come into my room. In her true kind and caring fashion, she brought me two coloring books and a box of crayons.

When my mother came to see me later that day, I told her about Mrs. Bowden's visit. She had the strangest look on her face. She did not believe me. After a series of questions and my mother's growing frustration, I finally showed her the coloring books Mrs. Bowden had brought me. My mother stopped her interrogation, sat back in her chair, and smiled. She told all my visitors that day about Mrs. Bowden. My mother showed them the coloring books, too. I did not understand the big deal about Mrs. Bowden coming to see me, but now I do. My appendectomy and Mrs. Bowden's visit occurred in 1965 during the height of the Civil Rights movement. The March on Washington was weeks away. The assassination of John F. Kennedy was still looming in the psyche of America. The Voting Rights Act was about to be signed into law. The ink on the Civil Rights Act of 1964 was not even dry. The 16th Street Baptist Church bombing in Birmingham killing three little black girls while in Sunday School had just horrified the nation. The Freedom Riders on Greyhound and Trailways buses were beaten throughout the South. Martin Luther King, Jr. had just written from a Birmingham jail. A&T University students were getting hot coffee poured on them at sit-ins. The Malcolm X Assassination had just taken place. Moreover, segregated schools, though illegal, were the norm.

These historical facts were what made Mrs. Bowden's visit monumental. She was white. My mother made us go to an all-white school, but a white schoolteacher coming to see a little black boy was more than my mother and family could believe. Had I not had the coloring books to prove it, no one would have believed me.

Mrs. Bowden showed kindness no matter what, and it was not just that day. She treated me like my white classmates. Coming to see me at the hospital was not about my color. It was about giving me what a sick child needed: coloring books and kindness.

The Contemporary Era

So, the sixties are long gone. Dr. King is long gone and buried. His dream for a race-blind society seems dead as well. So, where are we now?

Well, the contemporary scene for African Americans and the African American family is a rather mixed bag. We recently had an African American president, which is something for us to be proud of. Our forty-fourth president was, at least for a moment, allowed to be judged on the quality of his character, not the color of his skin. Dr. King would be proud of this accomplishment. But despite the presidency of Barack Obama, life for most African Americans is anything but presidential. Then, there is Donald Trump, who became the forty-fifth president and a complete repudiation of Barack Obama. America latched on to the dog whistle of "Make America Great Again" and voted in the exact opposite of President Obama.

What we are experiencing now is a culmination of all the stages that I talked about above. Because of a combination of the traditional African family structure and the impact of the counterculture of the sixties, the nuclear African American family is dissolving. In 2010, over seventy percent of African American children were born out of wedlock (*"Blacks Struggle with 72 Percent Unwed Mothers' Rate,"* N.B.C. News, 2010). Since one of the absolute best statistical predictors—and sociology has recently proven a causal, not a correlative relationship—of the trajectory of children's lives is the presence of both parents, the future of an entire generation of African American children—and especially the boys—is in profound question.

The drug culture of the sixties, which decimated the African American community, spawned a reaction in the eighties: the war on drugs. This war has cost our community a lot of casualties. As the N.A.A.C.P. notes, the statistics are horrifying. In general, between 1980 and 2015, the number of people in prison in the United States quadrupled, from 500,000 to over 2 million. Today, 1 in every 37 adults is in prison or under legal supervision. These numbers are approaching those of the former Soviet Union (N.A.A.C.P., 2017).

African Americans constitute thirty-four percent of the U.S. prison population. Perhaps the most staggering statistic that I will share with you is that almost ten percent of African American young men are in prison (N.A.A.C.P., 2017). Combine this statistic with two others and you will be truly horrified.

First, one of the fastest-growing industries in the United States is the private prison industry. Often private prisons will charge the state a lower fee if the state guarantees to fill prison beds. Thus, courts are incentivized to sentence people to prison. Second, since the 1990s, major metropolitan police forces have moved away from the concept of community policing in which officers see themselves as part of the community they patrol. The officer on the beat has replaced the rapid-response S.W.A.T. teams glamorized on television. This trend in policing and simply being black is reason enough to shoot first and ask questions later. Don't even get me started on the proliferation of African American men shot while their hands are up or shot in the back while running away from police.

There is nothing glamorous about the new policing style, which often involves the use of sniper rifles, gas masks, grenades, and even—I am not kidding—tanks. These S.W.A.T. teams are often used primarily in low-income African American neighborhoods like Jacksonville, Florida. The results of privatized prisons and militarized police forces have been devastating to African Americans.

If you think about it, we have moved into another kind of slavery. Police forces pick up African American males and chain them in prisons where they perform cheap labor for years on end—a new slavery. Our children end up being raised by their mothers who may be using drugs, or even extended families. These children, like the former slaves interviewed above, will never experience the love of a complete nuclear family.

So, the picture is not rosy. Not at all. Is it all hopeless? Not at all.

Throughout this book, we have discussed forming a fabulous family, one informed by the covenant family principles of grace, empowerment, intentionality, intimacy, and learning from life's lessons.

In the face of injustice—the beginning of the new slavery and dissolving families—these five principles are even more critical for the African American family. We cannot change the world overnight, but we can change ourselves to deal with that world in a way that empowers us, our family, and keeps us from being blown like leaves in the wind.

Given the unique history of African American families, becoming a fabulous family is even more challenging. That means employing the principles of a covenant family is crucial. African American families must have grace; our love must be deep and lasting. Our love must cover a multitude of faults and outlast the lingering problems of our past. We must be intentional, more so than other families, because the road is steeper and the battle more complex. The empowerment of our families' experience must reconnect us to our rich heritage. The fact that our ancestors survived slavery, the Civil War, Jim Crow laws, and denial of civil rights says our D.N.A. is full of perseverance and power. The intimacy of the African American family must be closer than close—whether extended family or immediate. The words that tie our family together must be tighter by our faith in Jesus Christ. Reframing our difficulties, mistakes, and missteps as stair steps instead of stumbling blocks is essential for us to keep moving forward. African American families are the epitome of a fabulous community bound together in covenant.

What Others are Saying

There is no doubt: Bishop Geoffrey Dudley is a force for our time. His untamed love for humanity, his openness and vulnerability in sharing his heart, make Family-ish stunning in its breadth and depth. This book is a treasury of lessons in living and loving.

Susan L. Taylor, Founder and CEO
National CARES Mentoring Movement
Editor-in-Chief Emerita
Essence Magazine

Great book! Anyone seriously interested in seeing their family thrive should read this book. Life changing.

Pastor Kendall Granger
Senior Pastor
New Life Community Church East St Louis IL

Every once in a while each of us is blessed to have a divine encounter with God that will change the trajectory of our destiny and leave a life-long impact on our life. You are holding in your hands what I believe to be an instrument of such an encounter with God. Dr. Geoffery Dudley has been used by the grace of Almighty God to put pen to paper, and release an offering that will shift your family, release generational favor and inspire the family to recognize the power of covenant with fresh revelation and insight. If you are serious about family, and becoming all that God has called you to be, then dedicate yourself to the principles found in this book.

Bishop Kim W. Brown
Mount Global Fellowship of Churches

Biography

Dr. Geoffrey V. Dudley, Sr. is from Goldsboro, NC and is the youngest of 11 children from the union of the late Bishop Leamon Dudley, Sr. the late Mrs. Ida Dorothy Dudley. He gave his life to Christ when he was 12 years old and began ministry at the early age of 13. Dr. Dudley is married to the former Glenda D. Jones of Spring Hope, NC. They have two children, Mahogany Kneecoal and Geoffrey Vincient II. He is a retired Air Force Chaplain Lieutenant Colonel, and in his 21 ½ years of service he has lived and ministered in many states and several countries. He diligently pursued formal education to prepare for a lifetime of ministry.

1981 – Bachelor of Arts, Communication, Drama & Speech, University of North Carolina at Greensboro

1991 – Master of Divinity, School of Theology, Virginia Union University

1992 – Master of Human Relations, University of Oklahoma

1997 – Post Master Education Specialist, University of Memphis

2000 – Doctor of Ministry, Samuel Dewitt Proctor School of Theology, Virginia Union University

2019 – Ph.D. Regent University

Dr. Dudley has Episcopal responsibility over several churches and ministries and coaches several pastors and leaders through Changing Lives Ministries. He has dedicated his life to serving the church and community through a variety of organizations. Dr. Dudley is the founding pastor of one of the fastest growing churches in the Metro East (O'Fallon, IL) area of St. Louis, MO, New Life In Christ Interdenominational Church. LifeChangers, as they call themselves, are committed to changing lives in their lifetime.

Dr. Dudley has also appeared on national news programs, having been on the Today Show, where they featured his family and his daughter going to college, and twice on the O'Reilly Factor, where he advised on the Michael Brown Shooting in Ferguson, MO. Bishop Dudley is widely regarded as an expert on the African American family.

CPSIA information can be obtained
at www.ICGtesting.com
Printed in the USA
BVHW061536281221
625047BV00015B/975

9 781940 786674